Wind strategy

SAIL
TO WIN

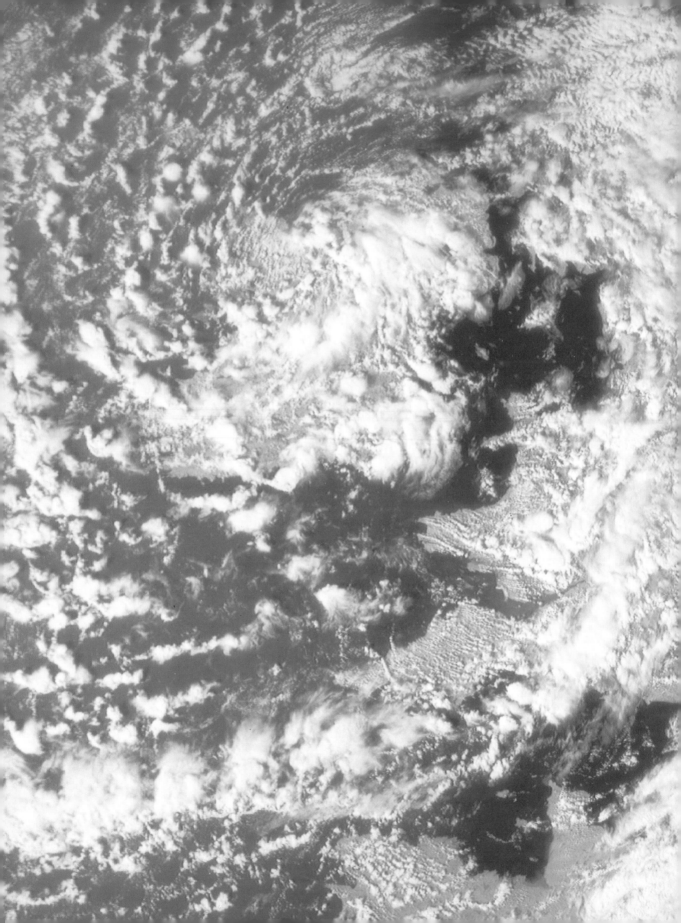

Wind strategy
David Houghton

Fernhurst Books

© David Houghton 1992

First edition published 1986 by Fernhurst Books,
33 Grand Parade, Brighton, East Sussex BN2 2QA

Printed and bound in Great Britain

British Library Cataloguing in Publication Data
Houghton, David
 Wind Strategy. - 2Rev. ed. - (Sail to Win Series)
I. Title II. Series
797.14

ISBN 0-906754-79-8

Acknowledgements
The publishers gratefully acknowledge permission to reproduce the photographs on the following pages. Paul Davies: page 73. Dept of Electrical Engineering and Electronics, University of Dundee: pages 2, 9, 14. Tim Hore: page 80. Kos: pages 13, 27 (bottom); cover. Ken Pilsbury FRPS: pages 27 (top), 35, 50, 60, 61, 63, 64, 66, 83. Francois Richard: page 31. Yachting Photographics: pages 7, 15, 16, 21, 33, 39, 43, 47, 75, 86.

Edited and designed by John Woodward
Artwork by Kirsten Blaikie and PanTek, Maidstone.
Cover design by Behram Kapadia and Simon Bally.
Composition by Central Southern Typesetters, Eastbourne.
Printed by Ebenezer Baylis & Son Ltd, Worcester.

Contents

Preface 6

1 The wind-wise sailor 7

2 The sailor's wind 9

3 Wind facts: coasts, islands and lakes 16

4 The open sea, water temperature and tide 23

5 Gusts and lulls 26

6 Wind facts: Southern Hemisphere 29

7 The sea breeze – pure and simple 34

8 Sea breeze with gradient wind 39

9 Afternoon winds: gradient wind onshore 44

10 Afternoon winds on lakes and peninsulas 48

11 As the sun goes down 51

12 Afternoon and evening winds
in the Southern Hemisphere 53

13 Mountain and valley winds,
gravity waves and billows 56

14 The message of the clouds 59

15 Obstacles in the wind 67

16 Currents 69

17 Waves 72

18 Weather routeing 75

19 Which sails? 78

20 At the regatta 81

21 Some popular venues 84

Index 92

Summary sheets for waterproofing
and taking afloat 93

PREFACE TO THE SECOND EDITION

Since the first edition of this book appeared eight years ago my experience with successive Olympic, Admiral's Cup, America's Cup and World Championship teams, plus the 1989–90 Whitbread round-the-world race, has honed and refined the concepts, arguments and rules of thumb it contains. Application of the principles to places like Auckland, Fremantle, Punta del Este, Barcelona, Dublin Bay, Travemunde and San Diego has revealed both strengths and weaknesses in the presentation; so has my dialogue with sailors and the subsequent search for an understanding of the bends and shifts which they observe.

The use of the information and ideas by the Met Office in the development of their meso-scale computer model has provided a totally independent judgement on the validity of some of the arguments, and my dialogue with Mike Cullen, now Director of Short-range Forecasting Research, has been particularly helpful. All this extra information has been taken into account in this second edition.

Major changes from the first edition are:
- The inclusion of information relevant to all hours rather than just the afternoon.
- A radically new discussion of how onshore winds vary during the day.
- More detailed guidance for the Southern Hemisphere.
- Case studies of particular venues.
- Summary pages for use on board.

I have managed to avoid mathematical equations, and have outlined the vagaries of the wind in terms which I hope most observers can relate to personal experience and appreciation of natural events.

Visiting some sailing venues for the first time at home and overseas I have been increasingly struck by how misleading local weather lore can be. Worth listening to, yes; useful intelligence, but not to be taken too literally. At a rough guess I would say that the description 'always' or 'invariably' applied to a local wind turns out to be right on approximately 45 per cent of occasions. When it turns out to be wrong the period of the regatta is subsequently described as 'unusual'.

Take Fremantle, for instance. "The Fremantle Doctor is totally reliable" we were told. "It always reaches about 25 knots". Yet on more than half the occasions during the Luis Vuitton and America's Cup series it was more like 15 knots. The reason for the difference between 15 knots on one day and 25 knots on another from approximately the same direction is explained in Chapters 9 and 12. It was predictable. And given the basic weather information normally available, the average sailor could predict it using the rules of thumb on pages 42, 43 and 45.

If you understand and use the information in these pages you should be able to apply it to any sailing venue, giving you an immediate advantage over other competitors who rely on local weather lore, enabling you to out-plan and outsail them on the water. That's wind strategy!

1 The wind-wise sailor

For the sailor every area of water has its own peculiar characteristics. The local helmsman has always been considered to have an advantage over the visitor because years of practice over the same stretch of water have given him a 'seat of the pants' appreciation of the vagaries of the local wind.

My role as meteorological adviser to our top helmsmen has been to help remove the visitors' disadvantage. Although every sailing venue is different, the forces which create the wind are in principle the same everywhere. There is a scientific reason for every windshift and bend, and virtually all those which are important to the sailor can be understood by the application of basic and straightforward principles of meteorology. This book is a result of over 20 years' study of a wide variety of coastal areas, working closely with sailors involved in world-class racing.

National Meteorological Services do not normally make observations in coastal waters. It is far too expensive. By and large the only observers are sailors, and it is their observations reported on the beach, in the bar and in the club house that have been the mainstay of my study. One might have thought that the picture would become more and more complex over the years, but the opposite has been the case. just a few basic principles have emerged which can be applied to winds virtually anywhere in the world.

The confidence of the 'seat of pants' sailor rests in the past. Every time he makes a decision about a windshift he argues "it happened last time", or if his catalogue is comprehensive "it happened in 19–". The confidence of the 'wind wise' sailor, on the other hand, rests in his appreciation of the causes of bends and bands in the wind, so that his experience at each venue increases his racing skill at subsequent venues. Because the weather demonstrates an almost infinite variety of variations there will always be some occasions when the 'seat of the pants' sailor is caught out – he hasn't seen it before. The 'wind wise' sailor, however, will identify a *reason* for the observed windshift and is likely to sail better through making well-founded decisions. He will not be right every time – that is hardly possible – but each observation increases his knowledge and helps build up a total picture of weather wisdom.

In 1960 I started teaching sailors how to use the wind, and at first I concentrated on the large scale of the weather map. We listened to the weather forecasts (in particular the early morning shipping forecast) and on the basis of our own weather maps we discussed the day's sailing to come. Each evening of the week's course at Falmouth we had a post mortem, and we became quite expert at using the shipping bulletins and making judgements on the behaviour of the large-scale weather systems – judgements which are of enormous benefit to the cruising sailor. But many questions were left unanswered. Why was the sea breeze so strong, so late, so weak, so variable? What did that black cloud mean? Each annual Weather and Sailing Course at Falmouth produced many observations which began to form the basis of simple models of wind behaviour.

Arising out of my experience with these courses I was invited to join the British team at the 1968 Mexico Olympics. Acapulco, site for the yachting events, was reputed to have unpredictable winds and currents. As is so often the case, the only weather observations were a small selection from the airport, an hour's drive from the city and even further from the sailing area. The Eastern Pacific Pilot provided some very general information based on the occasional observation from a passing ship within 200 kilometres of the coast.

I did what every sailor should do on arrival at a regatta: from the moment I landed in Acapulco I kept a systematic record of the wind and weather, both my own observations and those from every team boat. A sailing dinghy is a particularly good wind vane, but it took some time to get each helmsman used to reporting the wind in terms of the compass direction. During the two and a half weeks spent working up for the Olympic Games the winds and current began to fit into a recognisable pattern: the main features were a south-westerly sea breeze whose time of onset was related to the morning wind at between 1000 and 2000 metres (measured by balloon), and a 'slippery' sea: a shallow layer of very warm water which was propelled by the easterly land breeze during the night and reached speeds of up to 2 knots.

Kiel, venue for the 1972 yachting Olympics, proved a very difficult area to understand. We experienced wind directions from virtually every point of the compass, and my understanding of the sea breeze was inadequate to piece together all the observations we assembled before and during the Olympics. It proved to be the undoing of some team meteorologists.

Data gathered at the Kingston, Lake Ontario Olympics were particularly helpful in developing my understanding of sea breezes, and Tallinn, which I visited with the British team in 1978, provided a unique opportunity to study an area with a strong horizontal gradient in water temperature. Work with successive Admiral's Cup teams from 1971 and America's Cup teams from 1977, not to mention my own sailing, has provided a further wealth of experience of local winds in a number of areas. More data from other places will lead to a refinement of the ideas presented in this book, and there may even come a time when a computer can be fed details of the local area and the weather forecast and be asked to print out details of the winds to be expected over the racing area during the race. For the time being, however, we must be content with rules of thumb based on sound meteorological principles.

These principles are the same in both hemispheres, but most of the rules of thumb differ depending on whether you are north or south of the Equator. This book assumes for the most part that you are in the Northern Hemisphere. Differences applying in the Southern Hemisphere are covered, however, either immediately or in separate chapters.

Large-scale weather systems are explained in my book *Weather at Sea,* also published by Fernhurst Books, which includes guidance to the understanding, interpretation and construction of weather maps.

The weather map is useful for determining the pressure gradient wind, and the weather forecast will tell you the general surface wind. The shipping or coastal sea area bulletins give a very good estimate of the surface wind over the open sea. However, none of them includes details of modifications to the wind due to local effects (such as sea breezes or islands) and this is the purpose of my book – to help you work out, wherever in the world you are sailing, what the local wind will do and to understand any changes that may occur.

2 The sailor's wind

Anything moving requires energy to start it off, and in most cases to keep it going. The wind is no exception. Air moves around the world because the pressure, or weight of air is greater in some places than in others. And what causes this imbalance of pressure? Simply the fact that the sun heats some parts of the world more than others. If you turn to any geography textbook you will find a simple explanation of how on a global scale the preferential heating of the Equator creates the major wind systems of the world, hot air rising over the hot areas to be replaced by colder air moving in from the cold areas. The zone where the major warm and cold winds meet is commonly known as the polar front: the birthplace of many of the large weather systems of the temperate latitudes.

The traditional, and easiest way to map out the movements of air around the world is to show the distribution of atmospheric pressure at the Earth's surface. I say 'traditional' because weather maps with their lines of equal pressure – isobars – have been in use for over 100 years, ever since the invention of the electric telegraph. More recently, pictures from weather satellites have given greatly increased credibility to the concepts of cyclones, anticyclones and fronts, the clouds acting like dye in the air to map out these large-scale wind systems.

The pressure gradient wind

For wind details on the scale of tens to hundreds of kilometres there is still no substitute for the surface pressure pattern because there is a direct relationship between the wind and the gradient of surface pressure. Wherever there is a pressure gradient there is a wind whose strength is directly proportional to the gradient. On a non-rotating Earth the wind would blow directly from high to low pressure. But because of the Earth's rotation it blows *across* the pressure gradient, except near the Equator, one way in the Northern Hemisphere and the other way in the Southern. You can remember *which* way using Buy's Ballots Law which states that

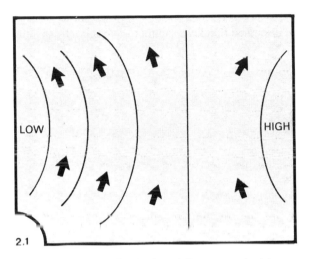

2.1

(for the Northern Hemisphere) if you stand with your back to the wind the low pressure is on your left-hand side (figure 2.1).

The pressure gradient wind is, if you like, the weather map wind – the wind which blows around areas of high and low pressure at a height of about 500 metres above the ground, sufficiently high not to be influenced by surface friction. Meteorologists call it the 'geostrophic (Earth turning) wind', but I will use the more readily understood name 'pressure gradient wind'. It is a real wind, and wherever there are low clouds you can observe it. One of the first things I do in the morning is to note the direction and judge the speed of any low cloud to assess the gradient wind. (A height of 500 to 700 metres is usually specified, but observing clouds anywhere between 300 and 1200 metres is usually good enough for practical purposes.) We shall see in the following chapters how knowing the gradient wind is the first stage in sorting out the characteristics of the surface wind near the coast.

Many weather maps have a scale in one corner called the 'geostrophic scale'. Figure 2.2 is an example. Using a pair of dividers, take the distance between adjacent isobars over the area of interest

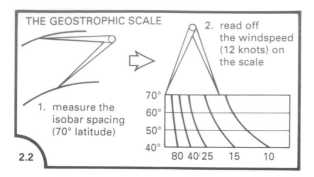

THE GEOSTROPHIC SCALE

1. measure the isobar spacing (70° latitude)

2. read off the windspeed (12 knots) on the scale

70°
60°
50°
40°

80 40 25   15   10

2.2

Opposite: satellite picture showing cloud systems with a depression south of Greenland and an anticyclone over N.W. Europe.

the gusts and lulls in which we constantly have to tack (see Chapter 5). You may also be able to make a reasonable shot at predicting the onset of a new breeze, or the next stage in the evolution of the one you have got. The purpose of this book is to make you a wind-wise sailor, capable of the best possible decision at every stage of a race.

and read off the wind speed for the appropriate latitude on the geostrophic scale. If you are sailing in different latitudes it is important to appreciate that, for a given isobar spacing, the wind is much stronger in low latitudes compared to high latitudes.

For a more detailed introduction to weather maps, weather systems and the balance between the pressure gradient and Earth-turning (Coriolis) forces see my companion book *Weather at Sea*.

Local winds
The global picture of the creation, movement and interaction of warm and cold air masses is repeated on virtually every scale down to that of the garden bonfire, where the hot air carries the smoke upwards and is replaced by colder air moving in around the sides (figure 2.3) If you can understand the general pattern of air movement around a bonfire you should be able to understand the local air movements due to the temperature differences between land and sea, often due to the heating of the land on a sunny day.

You can then contemplate the similar airflow into and out of a typical cumulus cloud, and the origin of

Drag and stability
We have mentioned how the pressure gradient drives the wind and how this pressure gradient wind is found at a height of about 500 metres, above the influence of surface drag or friction. We have also mentioned how air warmed at the ground rises to be replaced by colder air from aloft. The extent to which this happens depends upon the stability or buoyancy of the air, and this strongly influences the ability of the wind aloft to get down to the surface. Let's look at these factors in turn.

Drag   Drag can be fairly readily understood: the rougher the surface, the greater the drag. A smooth sea exerts minimum drag while a forest exerts near maximum drag.

Drag influences the speed of the wind. The greater the drag the slower the speed for a given pressure gradient. It also influences the direction, *backing* the wind from the pressure gradient direction in the Northern Hemisphere and *veering* it in the Southern Hemisphere. 'Backing' means the wind swings in an anticlockwise direction; 'veering' means the wind swings clockwise (figure 2.4). Over a smooth sea the direction changes by only about 15

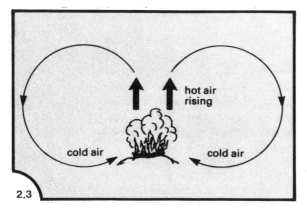

hot air rising

cold air   cold air

2.3

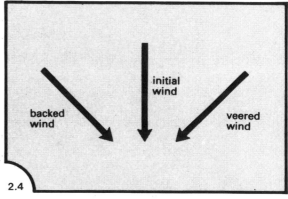

initial wind

backed wind   veered wind

2.4

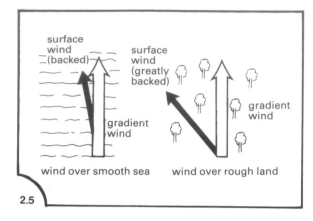

surface
wind ——
—(backed)—

surface
wind
(greatly
backed)

gradient
wind

gradient
wind

wind over smooth sea   wind over rough land

2.5

degrees, while over a forest the change may be 40 degrees or more (figure 2.5). The corresponding reductions in speed are about 10 per cent and 40 per cent, unless the air is stable.

Note that a modern town with a variety of high-rise buildings presents obstacles to the air flow rather than generating an overall friction or drag – see Chapter 15.

Stability   The critical factor in determining stability is the surface temperature. To overcome drag at the surface there has to be a continual transfer of momentum downwards; this process is seriously hindered when the air is stable, and encouraged when it is unstable (buoyant).

Air that is warmed at the surface becomes unstable and rises to be replaced by colder air from above. Air which is cooled becomes stable and resists any attempt to make it rise. Unstable air is continually overturning so that momentum is readily transferred downwards and the effect of friction at the surface is minimised. In stable air there is little interaction between the air near the surface and the air higher up; merely the drag of the air on itself which is insufficient to convey momentum downwards, so that frequently the air near the ground stops moving altogether (figure 2.6).

The visibility is a good indication of how well the air is mixed by overturning. In unstable air the visibility is typically good. In stable air pollution is trapped near the ground and it is typically hazy with relatively poor visibility.

Change in wind between day and night
Over land the rise and fall in temperature between day and night often causes major changes in the wind. There are of course sea breezes and land breezes. But there is also an inevitable change in stability of the air near the ground as it is heated or cooled by contact with the ground. During the day the air near the ground becomes increasingly unstable, and as the downward transfer of momentum increases so the wind increases, often to a maximum in mid-afternoon. As the sun goes down the temperature falls and the wind decreases. After dusk if there is little or no cloud the ground cools quickly, the air near it becomes colder and very stable and the surface wind soon dies.

If the wind is strong, 25 to 30 knots or more, there is usually enough mechanical turbulence to keep the air well mixed and maintain a downward transfer of momentum through the night as well as the day. This effectively prevents not only a fall in temperature at night but also a rise by day, and a more constant wind results.

On occasions when the wind dies away at night and cold stable air becomes established near the

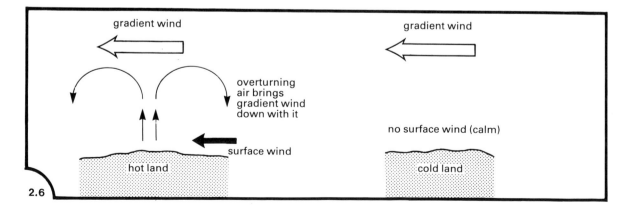

gradient wind

gradient wind

overturning
air brings
gradient wind
down with it

no surface wind (calm)

surface wind

hot land

cold land

2.6

surface over the land it can be very difficult to shift. Where the cold stable air is protected by hills from the wind above, for instance in an alpine valley, it can persist for two or three days and often needs cloud and rain to help to move it.

These considerations are important for inland sailors. The wind strength over a small lake is largely determined by what happens over the land around. Near coasts the influence of the changing land temperature will be very noticeable, especially if the gradient wind is offshore (see Chapters 3 and 8).

At sea the surface temperature varies little from day to night – a degree or two at most – since the specific heat of water is much greater than that of land. Under clear skies the change in wind between day and night is barely perceptible: a knot perhaps as the sea temperature changes by a degree or so. In fact variations in water temperature from place to place or due to changes in the tide may well have a greater influence on the wind.

Under skies covered with low cloud, however, a significant change in wind must be expected between day and night owing to the varying temperature of the top of the cloud. If the low cloud persists day and night the sea temperature will stay constant – there is no sun to warm it, and no clear sky to allow it to cool – but the top of the cloud will warm up by day and cool down at night. The colder the cloud top the greater the temperature drop from the sea surface to the top of the cloud, so the more unstable the air and the stronger the wind. The warmer the cloud top the smaller the temperature drop from the surface to the top of the cloud so the more stable the air and the lighter the wind (figure 2.7).

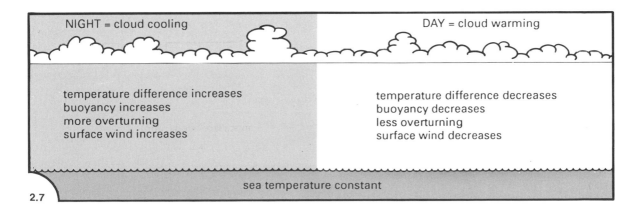

NIGHT = cloud cooling

DAY = cloud warming

temperature difference increases
buoyancy increases
more overturning
surface wind increases

temperature difference decreases
buoyancy decreases
less overturning
surface wind decreases

sea temperature constant

2.7

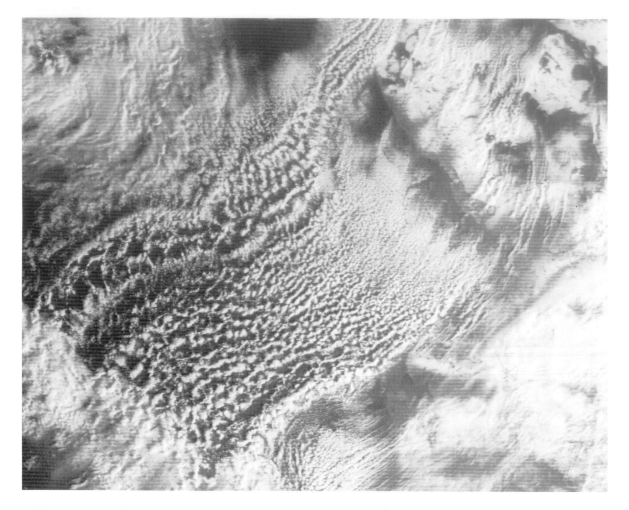

Above: satellite picture showing cumulus cells increasing in size downwind over a distance of about 800 kilometres. Sailors will experience associated regular windshifts at intervals increasing from ten minutes up to over an hour.

Hence under a sky covered in low cloud and with little or no cloud higher up – you may have to make an intelligent guess about that – the wind will be strongest in the early hours and lightest in the afternoon, so long as the pressure gradient is not changing. A good example is offshore at San Diego where over a cold sea there is often a persistent layer of stratocumulus and the average wind drops from about 13 knots in the early morning to between 6 and 8 knots in the afternoon.

Introducing gusts and lulls

So far we have described how the pressure gradient wind overcomes friction at the surface. We have seen that momentum is readily transferred downwards when the air is buoyant; given the slightest nudge through warming at the sea (or land)

surface the air will rise high enough to allow the colder and faster-moving air above to replace it at the surface. This overturning of the air often occurs in a regular pattern over the sea. Wherever there is a pocket of air moving down to the surface a gust of stronger wind is found. Where the air has spent longest near the sea surface, there is a lull; this is where the air is rising (figure 2.8). Cumulus clouds are visible evidence of this rising air. A cloud forms in each rising pocket of air, and between the clouds

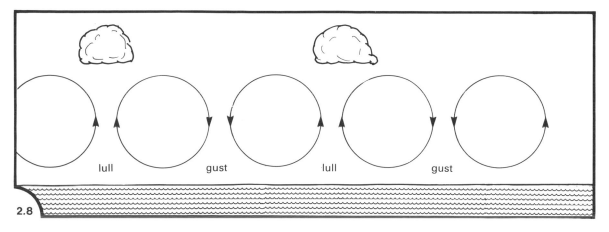

2.8

other invisible pockets of subsiding air are bringing the stronger winds from aloft down to the surface.

Overturning of the air also occurs on a much larger scale, characterised by clusters of cumulus or cumulonimbus clouds which satellite pictures show to be organised in cellular patterns varying from 50 km to nearly 300 km across.

The inference to be drawn from this is that regular patterns in the wind may be expected over the sea –

not often over the land because it is too rough – on a wide spectrum of time-scales of interest to the sailor, from one or two minutes upwards to an hour or two. Some periodicities are much more difficult to identify than others, but I have found in practice that every day has its own characteristic pattern of windshifts; the more clearly this pattern can be identified before a race the easier it will be to make decisions during that race.

3 Wind facts: coasts, islands and lakes

I have called this section 'Wind Facts' because I shall be describing bends and bands in the wind which are always present to some extent. They do not depend on the forecast, only on the orientation of the wind in relation to the land, the topography and the stability of the air.

Let us look first at the effect of the coast on the wind when the wind is blowing off, along and onto the shore. To start with we assume a coastline which is straight, or nearly so, and where the land is not particularly hilly; no cliffs or mountains within a few kilometres of the coast and no islands within at least 20 kilometres. The coast can be facing in any

Below: here the wind blowing along the coast (wind aft, coast on right-hand side) will give a zone of stronger wind inshore.

direction and the principles apply to any coast or shore whether sea or lake. Application to the Southern Hemisphere is the subject of Chapter 6.

Wind blowing off the shore

Some books state incorrectly that the bend in the wind as it leaves the coast is a case of refraction, and that the wind changes direction towards a line at right angles to the land. This is not so. We saw in Chapter 2 that the surface wind over land and water is angled at about 40 degrees and 15 degrees respectively back from the gradient wind. So whatever the angle of the wind to the shore, the direction must veer as it moves out over the water (figure 3.1). The speed of the wind increases at the same time.

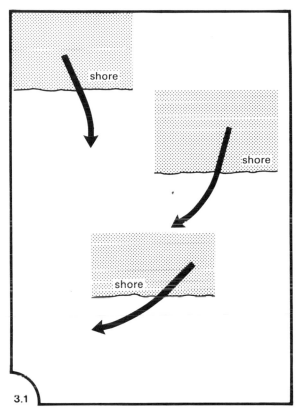

3.1

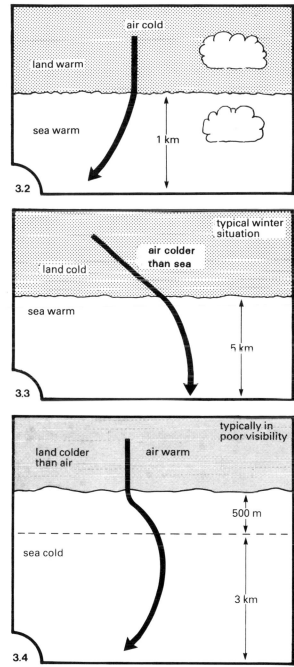

3.2

3.3

3.4

The veer is fairly gradual over a distance of from 1 to 5 km downwind from the shore, depending on the stability of the air (how quickly the moving air will adjust to the reduced friction over the sea).

If the air is cold and the sea and land are relatively warm (typically with cumulus clouds over both land and sea) the air is unstable to the temperatures of both land and sea surfaces and the veer in wind direction will be completed in a distance of about 1 kilometre downwind from the shore (figure 3.2).

If the land is cold, the sea warm, and the air relatively cold (a typical winter situation) the stability decreases as the air moves out over the water so the thermal mixing gradually gets going and the veer is likely to be completed in a distance of about 3 to 5 kilometres downwind (figure 3.3).

If the air is stable, that is, warm relative to both the land and sea temperature the change in direction as the wind leaves the land takes longer and is unlikely to be completed in less than 5 or 6 kilometres.

Just occasionally in this case the veer as the air leaves the shore is preceded by a sudden and short-lived back (figure 3.4). This occurs when the air is very stable: when the water is relatively cold, typically in poor visibility. The air then starts to slide

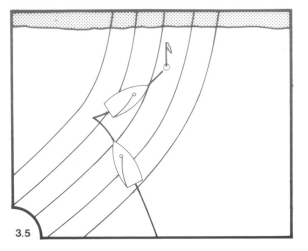

3.5

towards low pressure as it leaves the land, almost as though it was forgetting about the Coriolis Force. The back is likely to be more noticeable at masthead height than lower down.

Note that the relevant distance is the distance *downwind* from the coast, not the perpendicular distance from the coast. Also the wind direction we are talking about is the *average* wind direction, made up of both gusts and lulls and everything in between. The changes in the character of the gusts and lulls are discussed on page 28. The point to note here is that the change in wind direction will be most marked in the lulls.

In terms of tactics, if you are beating to a mark which is within 4 or 5 kilometres downwind from the coast you can expect port tack to pay (figure 3.5). The nearer you are to the coast the larger the bend in the wind, except for the relatively rare figure 3.4 situation.

Wind blowing along the shore

With a wind blowing parallel or nearly parallel to the coast there is a major difference in wind within about 10 km of the shore depending on whether the land is on the right or left hand when you are standing with your back to the wind. You will see from figure 3.6 that with the land on the right the different angles of the surface winds over land and water are convergent for the same pressure gradient wind, resulting in a band of stronger wind near the shore. The increase in speed in the band is of the order of 25 per cent, e.g. 5 knots added on to a 20-knot wind. One consequence of the converging airstreams is an increase in cloud near the coast, sometimes sufficient to produce a shower or two.

There is no precise figure for the distance from the shore of the strongest wind. On a straight coast it is generally between 1 and 5 km off. On an irregular coast the wind will blow so as to smooth out the irregularities. If for instance there are headlands separated by a shallow bay, the band of strong wind will extend from headland to headland, being close inshore at the headlands.

This stronger wind just offshore is sometimes mistaken for a sea breeze. In a recent race in the English Channel some boats headed out to sea off Brighton as dusk approached, assuming that the

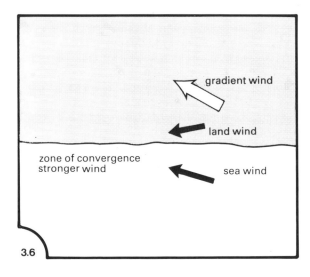

3.6

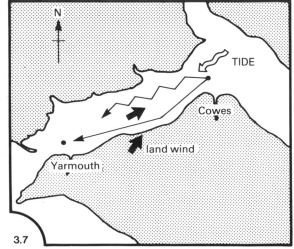

3.7

wind inshore was largely a sea breeze and would die away – only to find that those who stayed inshore benefited from an extra few knots of easterly wind all night.

If you are racing in a wind aligned in this way to the coast you can be reasonably sure not only of finding a strong wind band but also that it will remain in the same place throughout the race. Do not overlook the possible benefit of using the more backed, though lighter wind close to the shore where it will be coming off the land. In a recent Class One race in Cowes week, Yarmouth buoy could be made on a single tack close inshore (figure 3.7). Sailing in the more favourable tide a kilometre further off meant several tacks in a more veered south-westerly wind.

In the opposite case of the land on your left the two airstreams diverge (figure 3.8) and the wind is generally lighter within a few kilometres of the shore. Because of this divergence the air tends to subside near the coast and this clears, or at least thins any low cloud which may be around. This is why the sunniest seaside resorts are often found where the prevailing wind is westerly on a south facing coast, easterly on a north-facing coast and so on. The reduction in wind speed may be as much as 25 per cent compared to further offshore, but the position of the lightest wind in relation to the coast is rarely as clear-cut as in the case of the stronger wind in converging airstreams.

In the afternoon, particularly from late spring to early autumn, the reduction in wind is often

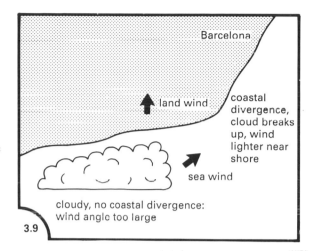

3.9

cancelled out by a thermal enhancement of the wind near the coast (see page 44). When racing at any other time this light-wind zone is normally to be avoided, though you might consider using a bend of up to 10 degrees towards the land which may be found close inshore (figure 3.8).

An interesting example of what happens at a bend in the coast was observed during the pre-Olympics at Barcelona in 1991. The wind was from 205 degrees true, and away to the south-west of Barcelona where the coast lies along 245 degrees there was a full cover of stratocumulus cloud at a height of about 500 metres. Some 7 kilometres south-west of the city where the coast bends to a new angle of about 210 degrees the cloud started to break up and by the time the wind reached Barcelona the skies were clear. The explanation for the cloud clearance was that when the coast became aligned at an angle within 20 degrees of the wind direction, the land wind and sea wind streamlines started diverging so that subsidence was induced near the shore and the cloud cleared (figure 3.9). For the sailor the change from cloudy to clear conveyed a message about the wind near the coast: 'Do not expect any variation in wind speed where it is cloudy. Look for a lighter wind zone where the cloud has cleared'.

In the 1973 Fastnet Race some yachts kept inshore on the south coast of England believing that with a ridge of high pressure in mid-Channel the wind would be lighter in the weaker pressure gradient further offshore. This was true for the most part, but the best wind was actually 10 kilometres out, just to seaward of the diverging airstreams near the English coast.

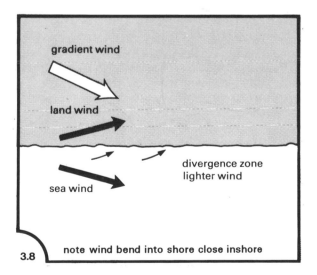

3.8

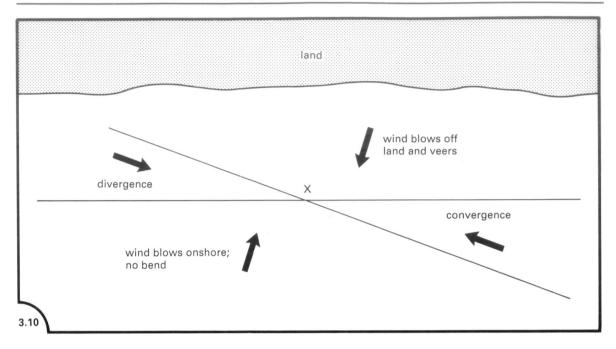

3.10

Wind blowing onto the shore

In this situation there is no significant variation in the wind strength or direction over the water as a result of the wind alignment to the shore. All the changes in wind characteristics occur over land. However, do not overlook the thermal effects created by the heating of the land in the afternoon which are described in Chapter 9.

Summary

Figure 3.10 summarises the influence of the land on winds over the adjacent water. Wind directions are those *over the water* relative to point X, the land being aligned as at the top of the diagram. The divisions between the zones of convergence and divergence will depend on whether or not the shoreline is reasonably straight. We shall see in Chapter 8 that these direction zones are also important in judging the likely development of the sea breeze.

Tactics

If it is wind you are looking for, then with the wind blowing along the shore, a course set within 5 kilometres of a straight coast and no overriding influence such as a sea breeze, you should stand well in or well off – depending upon the wind direction in relation to the coastline.

COASTAL CLIFFS

Wind blowing along the shore

If the wind is blowing along the coast and it is fairly straight, it makes little difference whether there are cliffs or not; the effects described above for the simple case are well marked and sometimes enhanced; i.e. we observe within a few kilometres of the coast a zone of stronger or lighter winds depending upon the wind direction. In the case of converging airstreams the strong wind band will be close to the cliffs.

Wind blowing off the shore

With the wind blowing off coastal cliffs, things are rather different. There is still the same veer in direction between the wind over the land and the wind well out to sea, but for at least 2 to 10 kilometres downwind (depending on the height of the cliffs) there may be standing waves and turbulence.

Standing waves form in the wind downwind of the cliff face when the air is stable or reasonably so, and they give relatively static zones of stronger and lighter wind, sometimes marked by a cloud sitting on top of the lighter wind zones (figure 3.11). The zones of stronger wind are the more reliable and are likely to remain in nearly the same place for as long as the

Above. when reaching parallel to cliffs, look for the zones of stronger wind in standing waves.

wind direction and stability of the airstream do not change, i.e. you can often expect them to stay put throughout the period of a race. The zones of lighter wind may be characterised by considerable variations – even reverses – in wind direction, particularly downwind of the higher cliffs, but the zones themselves are likely to stay put for some time. By careful steering you may be able to stay in a favourable zone, particularly when reaching parallel to a cliff.

Beneath the cliff itself there is usually a large eddy in the flow of air with a complete reversal in wind direction.

Above. when reaching parallel to cliffs, look for the zones of stronger wind in standing waves.

Wind blowing onto the shore

When the wind is blowing onto the shore there is usually a good deal of turbulence close to the cliff itself and it is advisable to keep reasonably well away from the cliff face. In a sea breeze situation (see Chapter 7) you should expect to find the sea breeze steered or bent into the nearest valley or break in the cliffs, depending on how high they are, i.e. blowing along the cliffs until the breeze finds an easier route into the land.

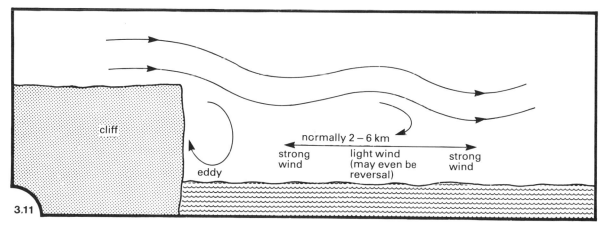

cliff

eddy

normally 2 – 6 km

strong wind

light wind (may even be reversal)

strong wind

3.11

ISLANDS AND LAKES

Islands and lakes of a size at least 5 or 6 kilometres along the wind direction are large enough to cause the full change in wind speed and direction due to the change in surface friction. They provide a neat summary of all the bends and bands in the wind which we have just been looking at.

An island

A mountainous island clearly obstructs the wind, and not surprisingly its influence extends many kilometres downwind. But even a small flat island has a significant influence on the wind up to 20 kilometres (or sometimes more) downwind.

A relatively flat island is fairly common. The air flowing over it is subject to greater friction so it slows down and its direction backs some 15 degrees; the time and distance over which this slowing and backing takes place depends on the stability of the air and the wind speed. Along one side of the island a zone of stronger wind will be evidence of converging airstreams and along the other side a zone of lighter wind evidence of diverging airstreams (figure 3.12). For the sailor it is particularly

important to recognise that these zones of stronger and lighter wind will not be limited to the island shore but will continue downwind for a considerable distance, perhaps tens of kilometres.

Within the 'shadow' of the island a bend will be found, caused simply by the wind blowing off the shore. However if the island is relatively high a back eddy is likely.

The most noticeable feature of mountainous islands are the vortices which are shed downwind. The Canaries are a good example. Satellite pictures often reveal vortex-shaped cloud patterns extending up to 300 to 400 kilometres downwind, each vortex being 50 or so kilometres across.

A lake

The pattern of wind follows all the principles we have just outlined. A lake in the order of a few kilometres across, such as Rutland Water or Grafham Water, is just big enough to demonstrate all of the main features: the bend downwind as the wind leaves the land (side A in figure 3.13); the convergence and stronger wind where the land is on the right-hand looking downwind (side C); and the divergence and lighter conditions where the land is on the left (side B). The case of a lake (sea) breeze is described in Chapter 7.

For much larger lakes it is likely that the gradient wind will be different on different coasts so that each section of coast will have to be looked at on its own. In the case of lakes or fjords surrounded by mountains you will need first to consider what difference the mountains are making to the gradient wind (see Chapter 13) before applying the guidelines of figure 3.13.

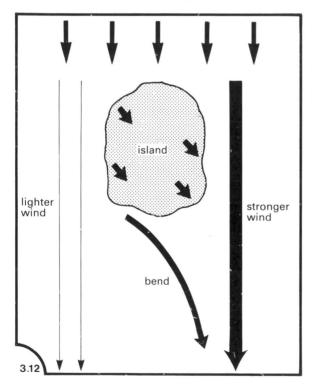

3.12

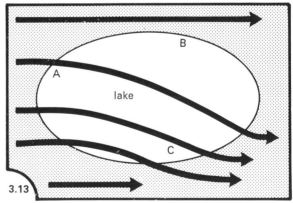

3.13

4 The open sea, water temperature and tide

THE OPEN SEA – WIND BANDS

It is a misconception to think of the wind being
uniform for a given pressure gradient. It is not, even
over a perfectly smooth sea – if such were possible.
The wind likes blowing in bands. The most striking
example of this is in the trade winds which are
characterised by lines of 'trade wind cumulus'
extending over hundreds of kilometres of open
ocean.

These lines of cloud are evidence of what are
called 'vortex rolls', where superimposed on the
horizontal motion of the air is a vertical circulation
of air moving slowly up into the line of cloud and
down into the clear lanes between. These cloud
lanes are typically 2 to 5 kilometres apart and the
wind somewhat stronger in the clear lanes than
under the clouds. A cross-section is shown in
figure 4.1.

Even in the absence of cloud, or beneath a
uniformly grey and cloudy sky, wind bands will be
found wherever wind is blowing over the open sea.
The difference in strength between adjacent light
and strong bands may be anything from 10 per cent

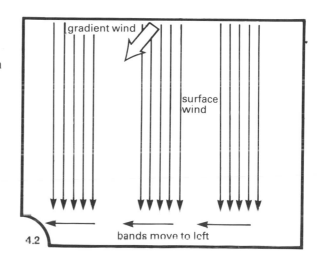

to 25 per cent, and their distance apart from 3 to 8
kilometres. Near the coast the position of the bands
will normally be fixed by some feature of the coast
or by the coastline itself, particularly when the wind
is nearly parallel to it. Well away from the coast, the
bands will move slowly due to the component of the
pressure gradient wind across them (figure 4.2).

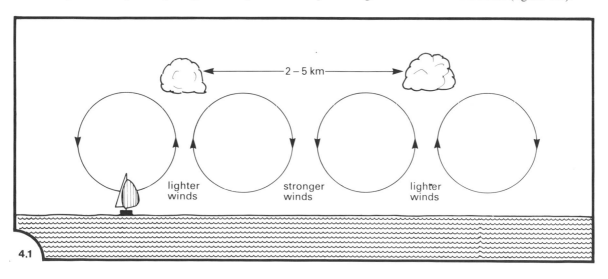

Thus if you are sailing on the open sea, at least 10 kilometres from land, and the wind is lighter than it should be, it is advisable to sail on port tack (or gybe) until you find the stronger wind. Having found it, change to starboard tack to enable you to stay in the stronger wind as long as possible. Adlard Coles wrote in the 1930s that in his experience when the breeze was dying it often paid to tack onto port to find fresher winds. Now we know why.

If the gradient wind is less than about 10 knots the bands tend to deform. And sometimes large eddies, 10 to 15 kilometres across, appear in the wind. These 'holes' move down the gradient wind, so if you find yourself nearly becalmed try to make way towards the gradient wind direction.

CHANGES IN WATER TEMPERATURE

A sudden change in water temperature of a few degrees is almost as significant as a coastline in influencing the wind. Over colder water the surface air will be cooled and become more stable; there will therefore be less vertical mixing and friction will cause the wind to back and slow down. Over warmer water the surface air will be warmed and become less stable; there will be more vertical mixing and the effect of friction will be more readily overcome, so that the wind will be stronger and more veered.

The zone or dividing line between cold and warm water will act like a coastline (figure 4.3). There will be a bend as the air moves from one to the other, the bend always on the side downwind of the transition.

For winds blowing along the transition a zone of convergence and stronger winds – or divergence and lighter winds – will be found, depending upon the direction; also the wind will be generally stronger over the warmer water than over the cold. But in the case of cold water on the right (back to wind) the zone of strongest wind may be just on the cold side of the boundary.

If the stability of the air is critical (i.e. the air is stable to the temperature over one area of water and unstable to the temperature over the adjacent area) the differences in wind speed between the two areas could be as high as 25 per cent; but the areas must be several kilometres across to be fully effective.

It is not uncommon to find water temperature changes of 4° or 5°C, particularly near estuaries, where the transition from one type of water to the other will be marked by a change in colour of the water surface.

Similar temperature differences may be found:
● Where there is tidal upwelling.
● When winds have been blowing onshore and pushed warm surface water towards the shore.
● When winds have been blowing offshore and pushed surface water away from the shore so that it is replaced by colder water from below.

None of these situations is unusual. Following a day or so of onshore or offshore winds variations in water temperature of 2° or 3°C can be experienced over a regatta course. If by the time of the regatta the wind has changed to an alongshore direction, the water temperature isotherms will be parallel to the

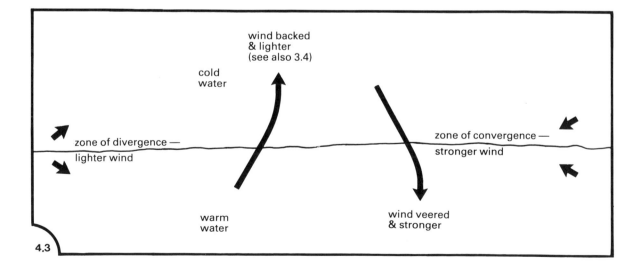

wind backed & lighter (see also 3.4)

cold water

zone of divergence — lighter wind

warm water

zone of convergence — stronger wind

wind veered & stronger

4.3

wind direction. There is then a strong chance that the course will straddle these isotherms so that the water on one side of the course will be noticeably warmer than on the other. Look for a stronger and more veered wind over the warmer water. This may not be very different from the situation near a river estuary which is discussed below.

Small horizontal temperature differences over the water surface may not be easy to recognise except by taking measurements with a thermometer, but even a difference of 1°C between one side of a course and the other will be significant in a closely fought race. It could mean at least an extra few per cent in wind speed.

THE TIDE

Changes in the tidal streams influence the wind in three ways:
- Through change in drag on the wind.
- Through changes in water temperature.
- Through changes in the temperature of the shore.

Change in drag on the wind
This effect is easy to appreciate. When the tide is running with the wind the drag of the water on the wind is less than normal for a given wind strength, particularly since the sea will be relatively smooth and the length of waves relatively long. A tidal stream running against the wind involves a considerable increase in drag, due both to the change in relative speed and the increase in height and steepness of the waves. The actual wind speed decreases and the direction backs a few degrees.

Change in water temperature
A change in tide is often accompanied by a change in water temperature, up or down depending on whether the ebb or flood is from a warmer or colder source, or as a consequence of upwelling of colder water from beneath. Colder water leads to colder air near the sea surface and thus increased stability, less tendency for thermally induced overturning and a lighter, more backed wind at the sea surface for a given pressure gradient wind. Warmer water leads to warmer air near the sea surface, decreased stability

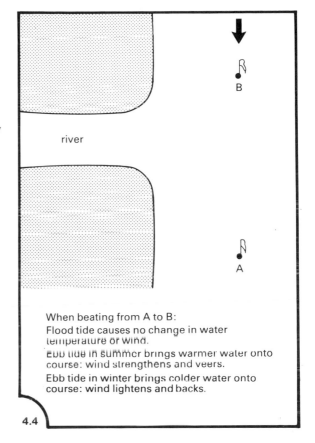

When beating from A to B:
Flood tide causes no change in water temperature or wind.
Ebb tide in summer brings warmer water onto course: wind strengthens and veers.
Ebb tide in winter brings colder water onto course: wind lightens and backs.

4.4

and a stronger, more veered wind for a given pressure gradient. So the clear message is: if you want the stronger and more veered wind, sail in the warmer water; if you want the lighter and more backed wind, sail in the colder water. The situation near an estuary is illustrated in figure 4.4.

Changes in shore temperature
The flooding by cold water of lage areas of sun-heated mud flats or sand changes significantly (and often suddenly) the local sea-breeze generating forces – see Chapter 7.

Changes in water temperature also influence the wind shear up the mast. This will depend on whether the water is warmer or colder than the air and by how much. See pages 12, 79 and 80.

5 Gusts and lulls

The wind varies on every timescale, from seconds to days or even longer. It is the short-period variations in the order of minutes which are normally described as gusts and lulls. We saw in Chapter 2 that these gusts and lulls are caused by air overturning near the sea or land surface so that the air aloft, which has not been slowed by friction, comes down to replace air which has been slowed. The most common cause of this overturning is thermal, that is when air warmed at the surface becomes buoyant, rises and has to be replaced by air from aloft.

On many days, particularly when there is a regular pattern of cumulus clouds, the gusts and lulls will arrive at fairly regular intervals. In these conditions the normal surface wind is blowing, but the air is also overturning, moving up underneath the clouds and down between them (figure 5.1).

The descending air has not experienced friction near the surface so it has approximately the horizontal speed and direction of the pressure gradient wind. It is significantly veered and stronger than the wind that has spent some time near the surface – in other words it is a gust. The air under each cloud has spent time near the surface and has slowed and backed, so it is a lull.

Time scale

If the cumulus clouds are small and relatively close together the time between the gusts and lulls will be quite short – perhaps 3 minutes or so. The wind will swing about 5 to 10 degrees between them and change by 5 to 10 per cent in speed. If the clouds are larger and further apart the time interval will be longer – perhaps 10 to 15 minutes – and the shifts may be less regular. If the convection becomes so deep that the cumulus clouds turn into cumulonimbus and showers develop, completely different wind characteristics result. They are described in Chapter 14.

Gusts and lulls at sea

Over the sea where the surface temperature is relatively uniform one usually finds fairly regular

Opposite, top: small cumulus clouds over land and sea typify fair weather, fresh winds and a short gust/lull pattern.
Opposite, bottom: when towering cumulus clouds, typical of unstable air, are also present pronounced gusts and lulls at longer intervals must also be expected.

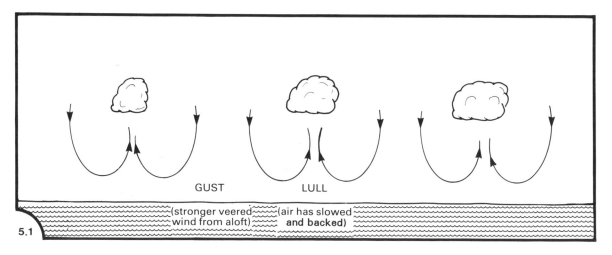

GUST   LULL

(stronger veered wind from aloft)   (air has slowed and backed)

5.1

patterns in the wind which can be timed and anticipated (figure 14.5). The most regular of all are in the Trades where row upon row of small cumulus clouds extend for hundreds of miles, each individual cloud indicating air rising beneath the cloud to be replaced by air moving downwards in the adjacent clear space.

Absence of cumulus clouds does not mean that there is no sequence of gusts and lulls, merely that the air is too dry for clouds to form.

Gusts and lulls inland

Over land the pattern of gusts and lulls is usually very irregular because the rise in temperature of the land surface depends on its colour and dryness, both of which vary greatly from place to place. Black tarmac, for instance, can be more than 10 degrees warmer than grass adjacent to it. Sailors on small inland lakes have to take the gusts and lulls as they come, but timing the gust/lull sequence can still be useful; the size and uniformity of any cumulus clouds provides an indication of their frequency and regularity.

The time of day is also relevant since, as the day progresses and the air warms up, the time interval between gusts becomes longer.

Gusts and lulls with offshore wind

An offshore wind carries with it the irregular arrangement of gusts and lulls experienced over land, but the pattern becomes gradually more regular as the wind settles down to blowing over the more uniform sea surface. We saw in Chapter 1 that this settling down takes from 1 to 5 kilometres downwind, and that the veer in wind as it moves offshore is most noticeable in the lulls, the gusts being closer to the gradient wind to start with. Again it is worth noting that, as the land warms up, the time interval between the gusts will increase until the pattern adjusts to the sea temperature.

Does the wind always veer in a gust?

The straight answer is "No!" Gust and veer, lull and back is the most commonly experienced pattern over the sea in the Northern Hemisphere for the reasons just described, and you can bank on it in moderate and fresh winds when the air is unstable as indicated by cumulus clouds. But there are occasions when:
● There is no preference – typically in stable air as indicated by poor visibility and low cloud, and when the wind is strong, causing turbulent mixing of the air that dominates and obscures any possible regular pattern of overturning.
● The gust will back. A backing gust on an inland water is just part of the greater variability of wind over land, but backing gusts over the open sea may be the first indication of a general back in the wind direction. Close to the coast they may suggest a bend in the wind towards the land.

Tactics

Before the start beat on one tack for a while and time the gusts/shifts – let's say there is a fairly regular period of 4 minutes between gusts. During the race watch for a gust approaching. Just before it strikes tack onto starboard – you will be lifted suddenly as the gust arrives. Carry on for 2 minutes; you will be slowly headed as you sail into the lull. Now tack onto port for 2 minutes to take advantage of the backed wind in the lull. As the next gust arrives, repeat the process.

Similarly on the run you will need to gybe as each header or lift arrives. Note that the interval will be slightly longer on the run. A good description of tacking and gybing on shifts is given in Rodney Pattisson's book *Tactics* in this series.

Squalls, billows and surface gravity currents

These could all be called gusts, but they are discussed elsewhere: squalls on page 60, billows and surface gravity currents on page 52.

6 Wind facts: Southern Hemisphere

All the features of the wind described in Chapters 2, 3, 4, and 5 are experienced in the Southern Hemisphere. The arguments are virtually identical, but because the influence of the Earth's rotation is reversed the wind blows in the opposite direction relative to the pressure gradient. Many of the relevant diagrams therefore are mirror images of those in the Northern Hemisphere. The following is a summary of the facts about the wind in the same sequence as was followed in Chapters 2 to 5.

Pressure gradient and surface winds, stability and friction

There is a pressure gradient wind which can be measured from the isobars using the same geostrophic scale (figure 2.2). Buy's Ballot's law for the Southern Hemisphere states that if you stand with your back to the wind low pressure will be to your right-hand side (figure 6.1). Because of friction the surface wind is slowed, but it is veered compared to the wind aloft, more so over land than over water (figure 6.2). The temperature of the land and sea relative to the air determines the buoyancy of the air and the ability of the wind aloft to get down to the surface. There is a diurnal variation in wind between day and night. Figures 2.3, 2.4, 2.6, 2.7, and 2.8 are

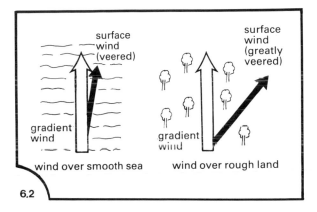

6.2

the same for both hemispheres. Gusts and lulls occur but a gust is a backed wind, and more backed than a lull.

COASTS, ISLANDS AND LAKES

Wind blowing offshore

The only diagram in Chapter 3 which applies equally in both hemispheres is figure 3.11. All the others are mirrored. As an offshore wind moves out over the water it backs and increases (figure 6.3), whatever the angle of the wind to the coast. The time (and

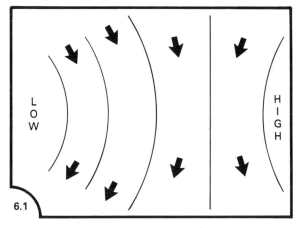

6.1

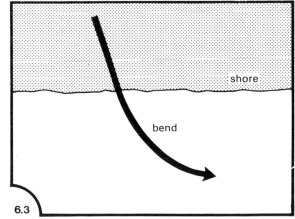

6.3

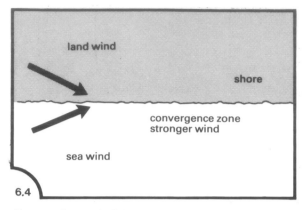

6.4

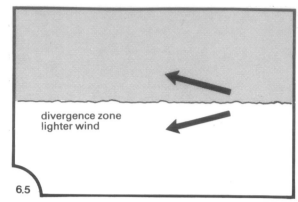

6.5

distance downwind) it takes for the new direction and speed to be fully realised depends on the stability of the air relative to the water temperature, as described on pages 12 and 17. The back is completed in about 1 km if the air is unstable – air cold, sea warm – and up to 5 km if the air is stable – air warm, sea relatively cold.

Wind blowing along the coast

When the wind is blowing along the coast, zones of convergence or divergence are found. The band of stronger wind features when the coast is on your left-hand side standing back to the wind (figure 6.4). The maximum wind will normally be experienced between 1 and 5 kilometres from the shore, but close to headlands on an irregular coast with shallow bays. The wind close to the shore will be relatively veered.

If the wind is blowing along the shore with the coast on your right-hand side there will be a band of lighter wind along the shore (figure 6.5); except in the afternoon from late spring to early autumn, when it is likely to be cancelled out by a thermal enhancement of the wind near the coast.

Summary: islands and lakes

Figure 6.6 summarises the influence of the land on winds over the adjacent water. Wind directions are those over the water relative to point X, the land being aligned as in the top of the diagram. The cases of an island (figure 6.7) and a lake (figure 6.8) also bring all the features together into one diagram.

The wind blowing over the island is slowed and veered, to give zones of convergence and divergence, and a back as the wind leaves the island.

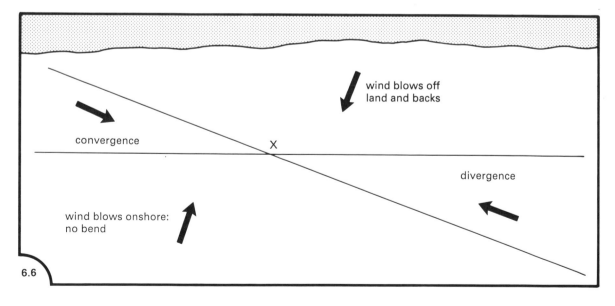

6.6

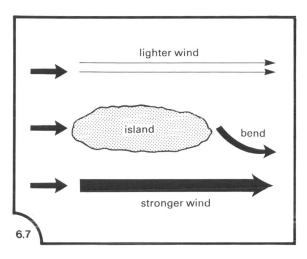

6.7

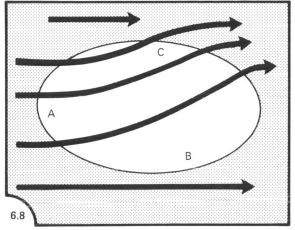

6.8

The bands of stronger and lighter wind often extend many kilometres downwind from the island.

Over a lake there is a back in direction downwind from the shore, a stronger wind on the left-hand shore looking downwind (C) and a lighter wind on the right-hand shore (B), the maximum effect in the case of a small lake being found near the downwind end.

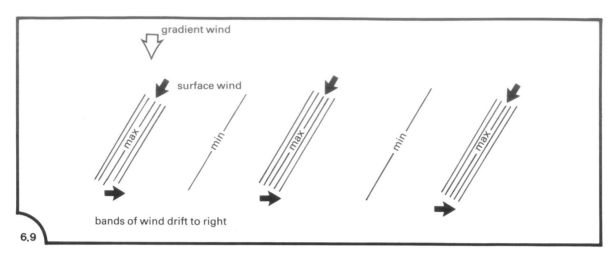

gradient wind

surface wind

max

min

max

min

max

bands of wind drift to right

6.9

THE OPEN SEA

Over the open sea you must expect wind bands. Figure 4.1 applies without amendment, but the direction of drift of the bands is reversed (figure 6.9). So if the wind is lighter than you think it should be, sail on starboard tack (or gybe) until you find the stronger wind, and then tack on to port to stay in it as long as possible.

Influence of water temperature
The changes in water temperature found near estuaries or at the meeting of different currents result in bends and bands in the wind in the same way as land-sea boundaries (figure 6.10). The wind is always relatively stronger and more backed over warmer water.

Gusts and lulls
The characteristics of gusts and lulls are identical except for the shift in direction. A gust is the stronger and more backed wind descending. A lull is the slower and veered wind which has spent the longest time suffering friction at the surface (figure 6.11). The back in direction downwind as a wind blows offshore is most noticeable in the lulls. The gusts, whether on land or sea, are relatively close to the gradient wind direction.

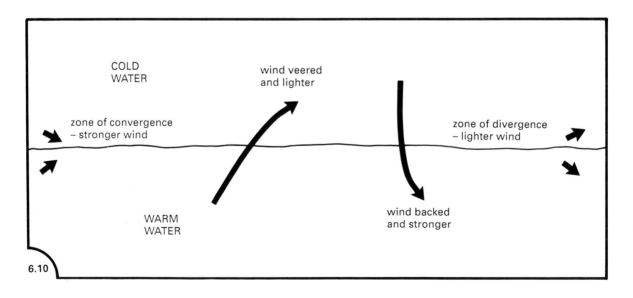

COLD
WATER

wind veered
and lighter

zone of convergence
– stronger wind

zone of divergence
– lighter wind

WARM
WATER

wind backed
and stronger

6.10

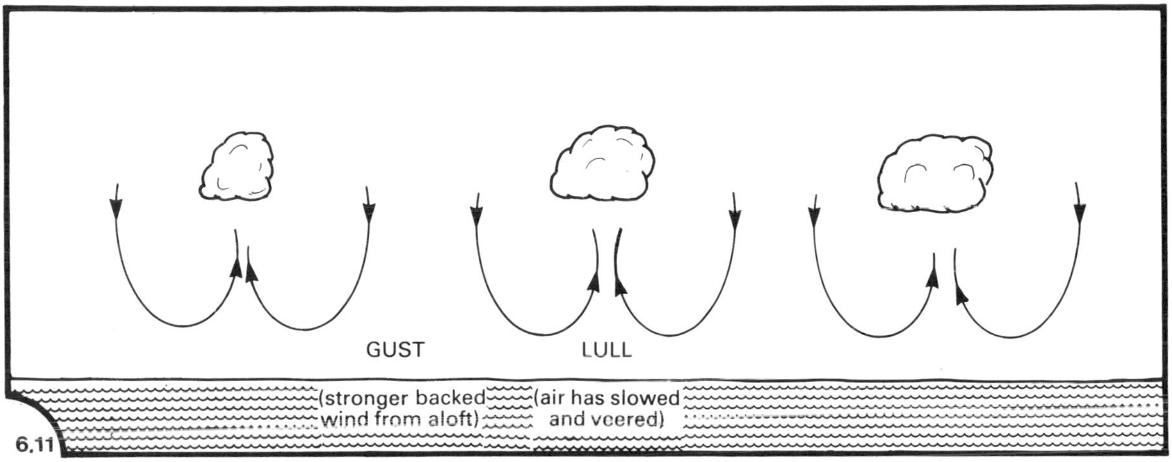

GUST
LULL
(stronger backed wind from aloft)
(air has slowed and veered)

6.11

F·9076
F.9076
F9085
F9085
87308
K-2546

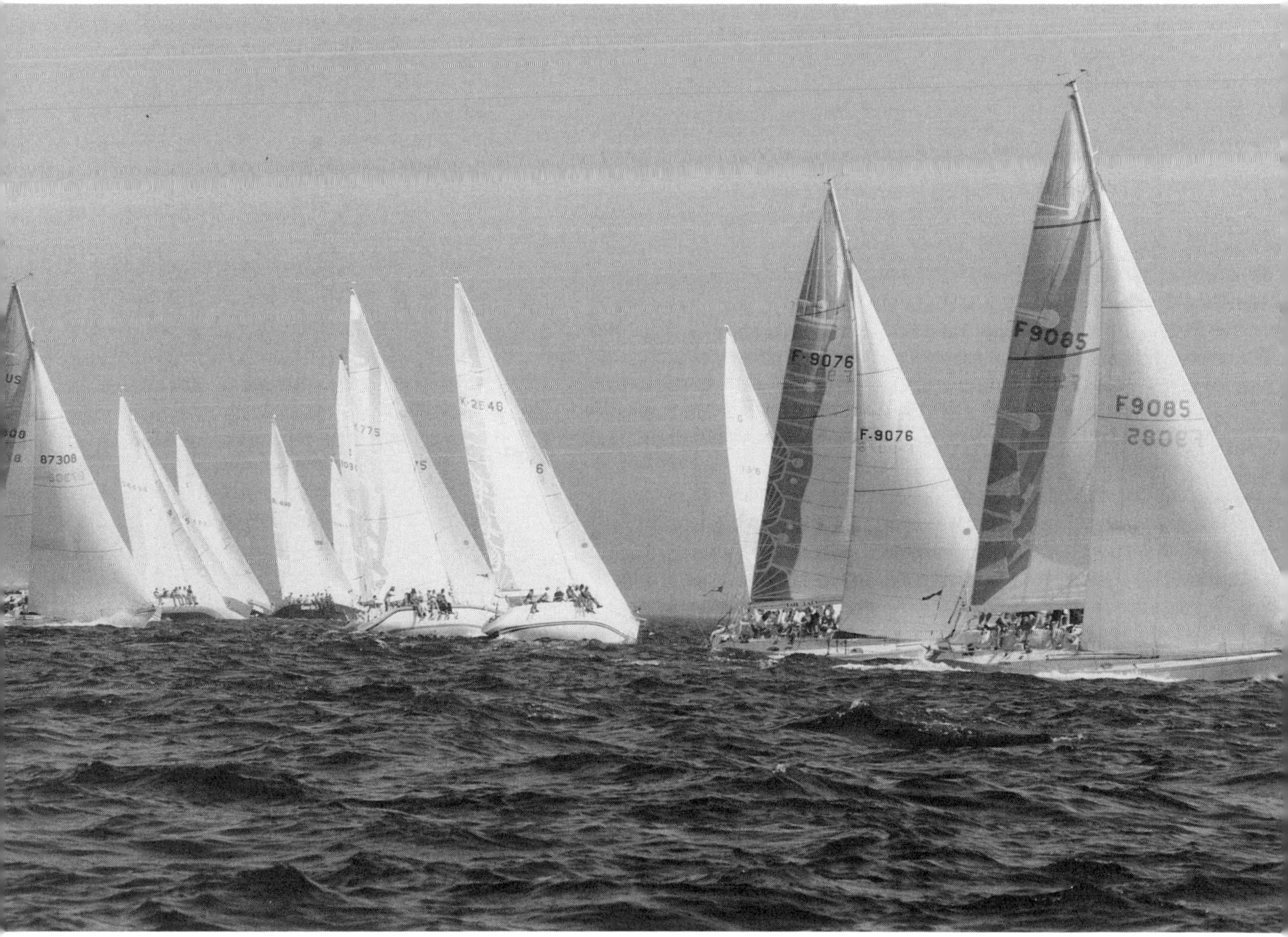

7 The sea breeze – pure and simple

The term 'sea breeze' is often used very loosely to describe any wind blowing onshore. But if we are to understand, recognise and use the changes in coastal winds which occur as the land warms we need more precise and meaningful definitions. In what follows the 'sea breeze' is identified as the wind which blows when the warming of the land during the day generates a closed circulation, with the air moving onshore near the surface being fed by air moving offshore a little higher up. This 'sea breeze' has very distinctive characteristics which are predictable and usable. Distinguishing between the sea breeze and other equally predictable onshore winds is essential to answering the question 'which side will pay?'

It is easier to introduce the behaviour of the sea breeze if we assume that there is no gradient wind. In the next chapter we will sort out what happens when there is a gradient wind, and how it either prevents or encourages a sea breeze.

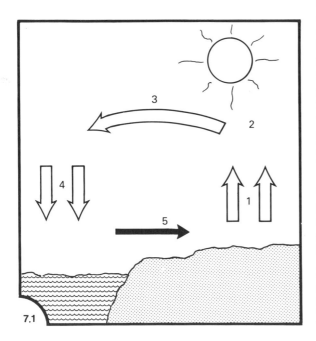

7.1

How it starts

The sea breeze is the result of air being warmed more over the land than over the sea. This can happen not only on a sunny day but also when there is thin or patchy cloud.

The first question to ask is 'will the air temperature over land be higher than over the sea?' If so, the sea breeze mechanism will begin to operate as follows (figure 7.1).

1 The air over the land is warmed and expands. A rise of 1° to 2°C over sea temperature is sufficient.
2 This causes an excess of air (an imbalance of pressure) at some higher level, usually between 300 and 1000 metres.
3 Air flows out seawards to remove the imbalance.
4 Air moves downwards (subsides) over the sea to take the place of air which is beginning to move across the shore. This is the sea breeze (5).

How far and how fast

As time goes on the sea breeze circulation, both onshore near the surface and offshore aloft, extends both inland and seawards. The further it extends seawards the more subsided air there is available to move inland; so the nearer you are to the coast the greater the quantity of subsided air moving towards the coast and the stronger the breeze. Typically you will find the breeze out to 50 or so kilometres by mid-afternoon with a speed increasing from 2 to 3 knots at the seaward extremity to 15 to 20 knots near the shore.

The final speed depends mainly on the stability of the air, because this determines the height of the return flow aloft. In the sort of stable air found in an anticyclone, typically when it is hazy, what is known as a subsidence inversion* acts as a lid on the sea breeze. The return flow can be confined to a ceiling

---

*In an anticylone air typically moves gradually downwards (subsides). Just as air cools when it rises it warms when it subsides. In an anticyclone, therefore, it is usual to find the air warmer at 500 metres or so than lower down – hence the term 'subsidence inversion'.

Above: line of cumulus forming just inland from the shore as the sea breeze starts.

as low as 500 metres, and with such limited room for the breeze to circulate, offshore as well as onshore, it will be weak with a maximum of some 10 knots. If the coast is mountainous and the 'lid' is below the tops of the mountains the return flow will be blocked by the mountains and any sea breeze will be confined to valleys.

The amount the land heats up is relatively unimportant to the development of the pure sea breeze, and this is one of the features which distinguishes it from other thermal influences on the wind discussed in Chapter 2.

Tactics
On a typical Olympic course with a race starting after the sea breeze has set in, the right-hand (landward) side of the course will always pay, the wind always being stronger nearer the shore.

Change in direction
Initially the sea breeze behaves as if air was being sucked into the shore, and its direction is at right angles to the coast. As the sea breeze circulation develops, more and more air arrives at the coast and starts to slide sideways, helped by the Earth's rotation which also determines which way it slides: towards the right in the Northern Hemisphere, and towards the left in the Southern. So having started blowing directly onshore, the breeze ends up blowing along the shore, at an angle of about 20 degrees from the shoreline, taking a shoreline direction averaged over about 10 kilometres. The veer (Northern Hemisphere) is fairly rapid in the first hour and is complete in 2 to 3 hours.

Tactics
Bank on a veer from the onset of the sea breeze, rapid at first then slowing down, until the wind angle is 20 degrees from the shoreline.

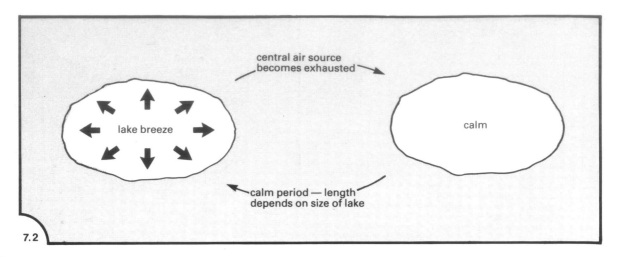

central air source
becomes exhausted

lake breeze

calm

calm period — length
depends on size of lake

7.2

Summary and signs

On a straight coastline and in the absence of any pressure gradient the sea breeze development proceeds as follows:

1 Calm morning, clear sky or fairly thin cloud (a full cover of stratocumulus [see Chapter 14] may not rule out a sea breeze).

2 Temperature over land rises above sea surface temperature.

3 Any cloud just offshore begins to disperse – a sign of subsidence starting.

4 Gentle drift of air onto coast from within about 1 kilometre offshore.

5 Breeze gradually increases and extends seawards. Cloud over land becomes more cumuliform.

6 Direction of breeze turns to the right (Northern Hemisphere), whichever direction the coast is facing. Typical change in the first hour is 40 degrees. Strength continues to increase, with the maximum always near the shore.

7 Final direction, about 20 degrees back from the shoreline, is achieved about 3 hours from the start. Speed increases until about mid-afternoon. Final strength depends mainly on stability of the air.

8 Breeze dies away towards sunset, depending on how quickly land temperature falls. Decrease most rapid near the shore where it was strongest. Light breeze may continue for a while out to sea.

COMPLICATED COASTLINES

Most coastlines are complicated, but by applying the basic principles outlined above to some typical situations you should be able to work out for yourself the likely sea breeze in any other situation which you encounter. It is still assumed there is no pressure gradient and therefore no existing wind to complicate matters.

A lake So far as the driving mechanism is concerned there is no difference between a sea breeze and a lake breeze. Consider an average sized lake, say 5 to 30 kilometres across (figure 7.2).

1 The lake breeze starts as a drift of air onto all shores with subsidence over the whole central area.

2 Subsidence limited to the relatively small central area of the lake proves insufficient to feed breeze onto all shores: as the source of air is exhausted the breeze dies away.

3 After a calm period the lake breeze begins again.

4 As the central air source is exhausted, so it grows calm again.

This cycle is repeated every 15 minutes to 2 hours or so, the time depending on the size of the lake. If the lake is very large the source of subsiding air may be regarded as unlimited and the sea breeze will operate as for a normal sea coast.

A large bay with a narrow opening At first the sea breeze is a drift of air onto all the shores (figure 7.3). The onshore breezes in the bay have difficulty finding enough air to feed them and their strength pulsates between calm and 2 or 3 knots as with the lake breeze. However there is also an increase in the pull of air through the entrance to the bay and this is in the same direction as the sea breeze onto the main shore, i.e. onto the straighter part of the coastline.

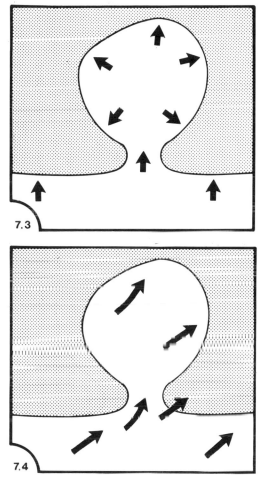

7.3

7.4

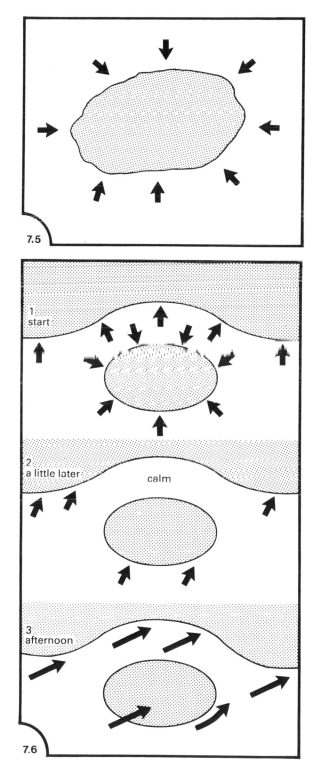

7.5

7.6

Thus after 2 to 3 hours the breeze has changed as shown in figure 7.4.

The sea breeze soon extends well inland and the gradual veer during the day means that for most of the time the right-hand shore of the bay is favoured. The breeze in the entrance is likely to be somewhat stronger than elsewhere with a tendency for convergence of air into the entrance and a bend in the wind on the right-hand side.

An island This is the opposite situation to a lake: there is plenty of air to feed the sea breeze, but hardly anywhere for it to go. If the island were perfectly flat and uniform there would be a gentle onshore breeze all round and perhaps a cloud sitting over the middle (figure 7.5). The breeze will pulsate a little, veer somewhat during the day, and its strength will depend on the size of the island. In

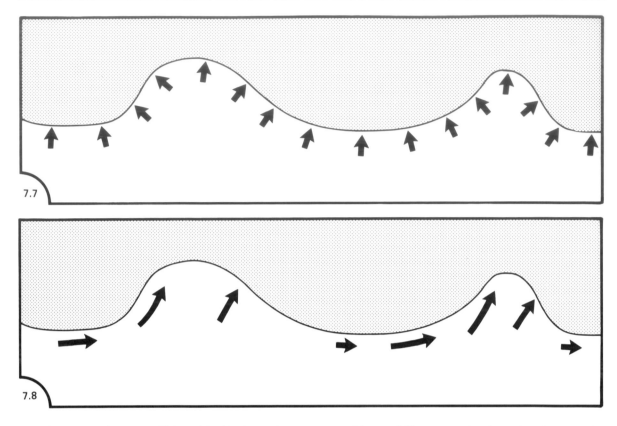

7.7

7.8

practice the sea breezes will be critically dependent on the topography, and even small hills, bays and valleys will cause good local breezes at the expense of calms elsewhere.

An island near the mainland In this case the mainland sea breeze will gradually take over and eventually swamp the more local breezes on to the island, though not before there have been successive stages of light wind and calm over the more enclosed area of water as breezes try to blow onto all shores. The pattern is shown in figure 7.6.

A mountainous coast with valleys The sea breeze will start to blow on to all the shores in the normal way (figure 7.7) up the hillsides as well as into the valleys. But gradually the breeze into the valleys is likely to dominate (figure 7.8) and may reach 20 knots. However, if the hilltops extend into the subsidence inversion and prevent the return flow aloft even the valley breeze will be limited to Force 2 or 3. During the practice races for the 1988 Olympics in Pusan, South Korea a potentially good sea breeze

turned into a drift as an anticyclone developed and its inversion dropped below the tops of the 300 to 600 metre mountains near the coast.

Warm and cold water
The colder the water the greater the encouragement to subsidence. One would therefore expect to find a sea breeze tending to emanate from the colder water, if there is a choice. I have observed this off Rhode Island when on occasions the sea breeze seems to start from an area of much colder water some 20 kilometres to the southeast of Newport.

Summary
So we see that, as a general rule, for any coast, however complicated, and whatever direction it faces, the sea breeze will always start as a gentle breeze onshore and then develop into a fresh breeze whose direction largely irons out at least the minor pecularities of the coastline. As it does so the breeze veers until it blows from a final direction approximately 20 degrees to seaward from the overall line of the coast.

8 Sea breeze with gradient wind

We can now see how the generation of a sea breeze is affected by a gradient wind already blowing. We have seen that two essential components of the sea breeze circulation are:
- An opposite (offshore) breeze blowing at some height aloft.
- The subsidence of air offshore.

In the absence of a pressure gradient there is no hindrance (or help) to either of these components and a sea breeze develops whenever the temperature of the land rises from a value below to a value above the sea surface temperature.

How important is the temperature?

Many people think that a warm sunny day at the seaside is invariably a situation for a sea breeze, but this is not so. Take for instance Cowes Week 1982. The sea was cool (temperature about 17°C), the air was warm (temperature in the 20s), but for two days there was virtually no wind and no racing. Why?

And what about Mediterranean coasts in summer? Some experience sea breezes and some do not. I well remember when working with the British Team at Kiel in preparation for the 1972 Olympics recording over 15 knots of sea breeze one day and less than 3 knots the following day, which was warmer. This was before I had discovered what controlled the sea breeze. I had expected an even better breeze on the warmer day and in the event there was barely enough wind to sail. The key factor every time and in every place is the pressure gradient wind.

Gradient wind direction

The sea breeze does not require a large rise in temperature to start it blowing – 2 or 3 degrees is ample – but it is critically dependent on whether or not the gradient wind is blowing offshore. An offshore wind helps the return flow of the sea breeze aloft and, so long as it is not too strong – 25 knots is the upper limit – the sea breeze has no problem tucking in near the ground beneath the opposite wind aloft. If the gradient wind is blowing onshore it opposes the return flow which is needed to supply the surface sea breeze, and a true sea breeze does not develop. What happens is considered separately in Chapter 9.

Given an offshore gradient wind, the way the sea breeze develops over the water also depends on whether this gradient wind has a component from left to right or right to left along the coast. With a component from left to right there is a tendency for the surface wind streamlines to diverge which encourages subsidence (look back to figure 3.8). Encouraging subsidence encourages the sea breeze which depends on subsidence to feed it. By contrast, if the gradient wind has a component from right to left the surface wind streamlines converge and subsidence over the water is discouraged. These considerations – offshore versus onshore wind, and diverging versus converging streamlines – provide the essence of a simple sea breeze model.

Sea breeze model

To estimate both the likelihood and the character of
the sea breeze for any coastline anywhere in the
Northern Hemisphere, imagine a line drawn at right
angles to the coast. The four quadrants created by
this represent four ranges of direction of the
gradient wind (figure 8.1). We will now look in detail
at what happens when the gradient wind is in
quadrants 1 and 2. Winds in quadrants 3 and 4
oppose the development of a genuine sea breeze,
and are considered in Chapter 9.

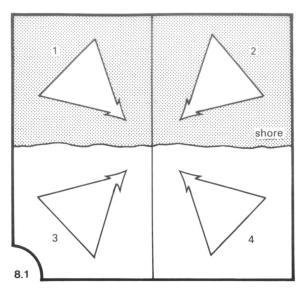

8.1

Quadrant 1   Quadrant 1 is the range of gradient
wind directions for the best sea breezes; in relation
to the lie of the coast these wind directions are
between west and north on a south-facing coast,
south and west on an east-facing coast, and so on. I
have known breezes to reach a good 20 knots or
more when the pressure gradient wind is in this
quadrant.

 The normal sequence of events starts with an early
morning wind blowing offshore, then as the land
warms up this wind dies away inshore and an
onshore breeze starts, usually before mid-day. It
increases steadily over the next 2 to 3 hours, extends
20 to 30 kilometres seawards, and veers, quickly at
first then more slowly, until it is blowing about 20
degrees back from the direction parallel to the
coast (plan view figure 8.2). The calm which
precedes the new breeze moves out seawards ahead
of it, a zone of virtually no wind 100 to 300 metres
wide. The sea breeze will be strongest inshore at
every stage, and lightest at its seaward extremity.

 If the initial surface wind direction is nearly
parallel to the coast the onset of the sea breeze will
merely back the wind near the shore rather than kill
it altogether (figure 8.3); this backed wind will
extend gradually seawards and veer to the final sea
breeze direction, 20 degrees back from the coastline.

Quadrant 2   In quadrant 2 we are talking about
gradient winds between north and east on a south-
facing coast, south and west on a north-facing coast,
and all directions in between. There is an offshore
component of wind to help the sea breeze but,
particularly for winds nearly parallel to the coast,
the problem of the convergence of airstreams near

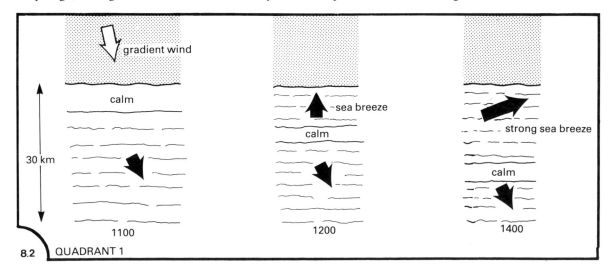

8.2   QUADRANT 1

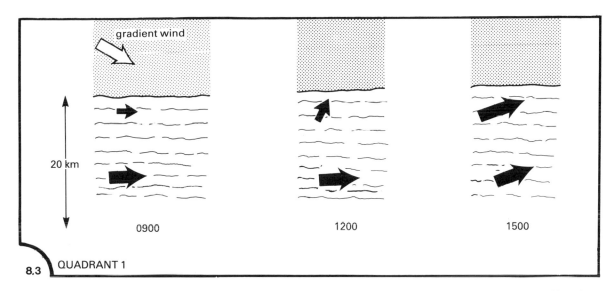

8.3 QUADRANT 1

the shore inhibits subsidence (see figure 3.6). In practice the sea breeze finds an interesting way of overcoming this problem. It starts up to seaward of the zone of convergence, several kilometres from the shore, and slowly moves in towards the shore as it develops (plan view figure 8.4); the nearer the

gradient wind is to blowing along the shoreline the further seawards the sea breeze may start. We then have the interesting phenomenon of boats beating in opposite directions towards the same point.

The zone where the two winds converge is usually half to one kilometre wide, with no wind at all or

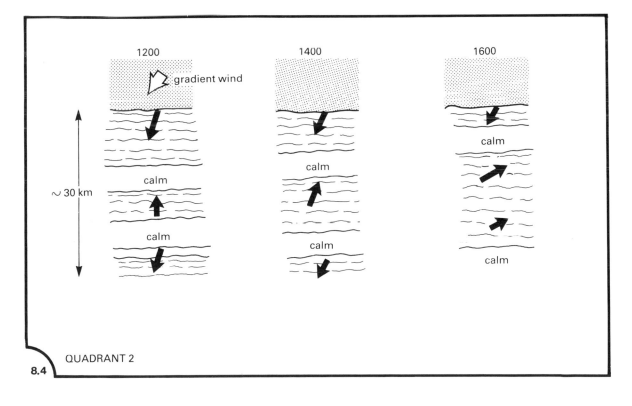

8.4 QUADRANT 2

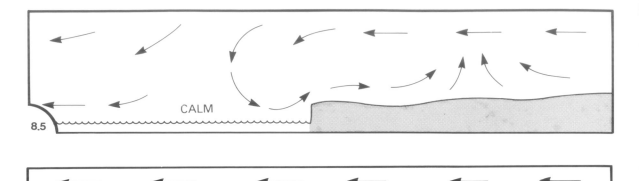

8.5

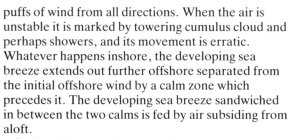

8.6

puffs of wind from all directions. When the air is unstable it is marked by towering cumulus cloud and perhaps showers, and its movement is erratic. Whatever happens inshore, the developing sea breeze extends out further offshore separated from the initial offshore wind by a calm zone which precedes it. The developing sea breeze sandwiched in between the two calms is fed by air subsiding from aloft.

In the sixth race of the 1976 Olympics at Kingston, Ontario the gradient wind, a north-easterly, was in this quadrant. A south-westerly sea breeze moved in from seaward during the afternoon but since it reached only one of the courses racing was abandoned.

Sea breeze calm zones

An important feature of the genuine sea breeze is the temporary zone of calm or very light winds which separates the initial offshore gradient wind from the newly developing sea breeze. Figures 8.5 and 8.6 help you to visualise them in cross section. For gradient winds in quadrant 1 (figure 8.5) there is a single calm zone which starts close to the shore and moves out seawards at from 5 to 10 knots.

For gradient winds in quadrant 2 when the sea breeze starts some distance seaward from the coast there are two calm zones (figure 8.6). The most seaward calm moves out to sea as in the quadrant 1 case though rather more slowly. The inshore calm

moves slowly towards the shore. If the gradient wind is more than about 40 degrees from the shoreline (sector 2A figure 8.7) the sea breeze will cross the coast and move inland. If the gradient is within about 40 degrees of the shoreline (sector 2B figure 8.7) the sea breeze is likely to stay just offshore, its position depending on coastal features such as bays and estuaries. For instance with an east-north-easterly gradient in the east Solent on the south coast of England the calm zone, typically marked by threatening-looking cumulus clouds, may stay offshore from Selsey Bill but move some distance north up the east Solent.

Strength, direction and signs

The sea breeze which develops with gradient winds in quadrants 1 and 2 has all the same characteristics as the pure and simple sea breeze described in Chapter 7.

Strength It increases steadily from a gentle start and is always strongest near the shore, reaching a maximum by mid-afternoon and dying towards dusk. The final strength depends on the stability of the air. With a quadrant 1 gradient wind and fresh cold air following a cold front it can reach 25 knots. If the depth of the sea breeze cell is limited by an anticyclonic temperature inversion, typically in hazy conditions (see pages 12 and 34), 10 to 15 knots is more likely.

Direction It starts blowing onshore, veers fairly quickly in the first hour or so and achieves a final direction about 20 degrees back from the shoreline within about 3 hours. In low latitudes the swing is rather slower and the final angle to the shore is some 10 to 20 degrees greater.

Signs Dispersal of low cloud just offshore, or to seaward of the coastal convergence in the case of a quadrant 2 wind, heralds the start of the sea breeze. Development of cumulus over land is also a good sign.

Tactics

On a typical Olympic course with a race starting after the sea breeze has set in, the right hand (landward) side of the course will always pay, the wind being stronger near the shore.

Bank on a veer from the onset of the sea breeze, rapid at first then slowing down, until the wind angle is 20 degrees back from the shoreline.

Marginal cases

Gradient wind over 20 knots In my experience 25 knots of offshore wind is the upper limit for a sea breeze to develop. But between 20 and 25 knots it may or may not develop depending whether everything else is just right. It is more likely when the wind is in quadrant 1 and the coast is flat. On an undulating coast you may find the sea breeze blowing onto one part of the coast side by side with the offshore wind. The two winds were experienced like this on an inshore Admirals Cup course in Christchurch Bay in 1989.

Gradient wind nearly parallel to the coast Turn to the end of Chapter 9.

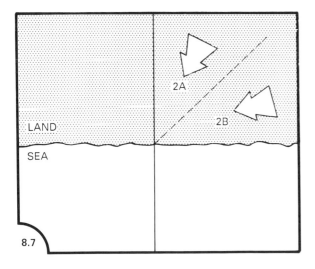

9 Afternoon winds: gradient wind onshore

Coastal winds when the gradient wind is onshore also respond to afternoon heating of the nearby land, but not in the same way as I have described in Chapters 7 and 8. The evolution of the wind from morning through to afternoon is different in both speed and direction, and if you do not discriminate between the onshore wind and the genuine sea breeze of Chapters 7 and 8 you are unlikely to adopt the right sailing tactics. Confusing an onshore gradient wind with a sea breeze is likely to be more of a hindrance than a help. It does sometimes veer and increase like a sea breeze, but sometimes it does the opposite; it is important to know why and when.

We will split the range of wind directions into two further quadrants, this time 3 and 4 (figure 9.1); because this enables us to discriminate between the coastal divergence situation, with land on the left hand standing back to the wind (see figure 3.8) when the wind is normally relatively light near the shore, and the coastal convergence situation (figure 3.6) when a band of stronger wind can be expected near the shore.

Two points worth noting at this stage of the discussion are that:
• The afternoon heating of the land operates against the coastal divergence and convergence effects, augmenting the quadrant 3 wind and reducing the quadrant 4 wind.
• The hotter the land becomes the greater its effect on the wind, by contrast to the genuine sea breeze which is relatively independent of how high the temperature rises.

QUADRANT 3

A quadrant 3 gradient wind is a south-westerly wind on a south-facing coast, a north-easterly on a north-facing coast, and so on. When the wind is in this quadrant the pressure must be relatively low over the land. Since heating of the land during the day causes the pressure over the land to fall, the low gets lower; and since the pressure over the sea stays the same the pressure gradient increases and the wind must increase. The fall in pressure over land between mid-morning and mid-afternoon is typically 2 to 5 millibars; the greater the rise in temperature the greater the fall in pressure.

Translated onto the weather map this is the same as bending the isobars towards the coast (figure 9.2) – notice how much closer together they become near the coast. In wind terms this means an extra component of gradient wind near the coast and parallel to it, which gives an extra component of surface wind from a direction about 15 degrees back from the shoreline. I will call it the thermal component.

Change in speed and direction
The change in the onshore wind as the land heats up depends on the relative strength and direction of the gradient wind and the thermal component. If the initial gradient wind is strong it will remain the dominant wind and the change in direction will be

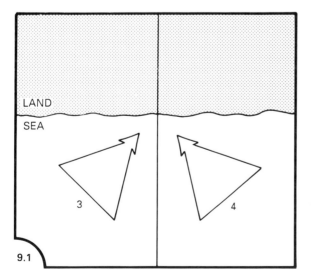

9.1
LAND
SEA
3
4

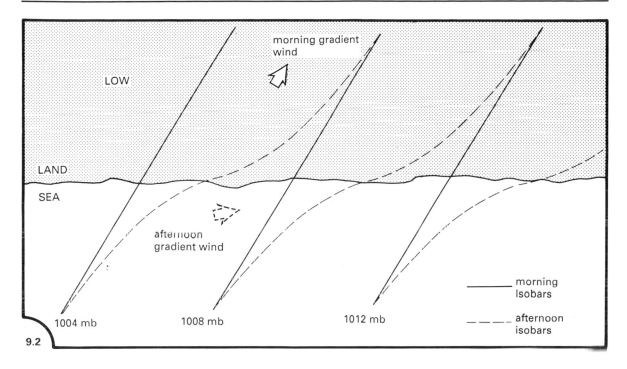

morning gradient wind

LOW

LAND

SEA

afternoon gradient wind

1004 mb   1008 mb   1012 mb

—————— morning Isobars

— — — — afternoon isobars

9.2

small. If the gradient wind is light the veer due to heating will be relatively more important and the afternoon wind will approach a direction 15 degrees back from the shoreline. To work it out in more detail you can either add the two vectors, the pressure gradient wind and the thermal; or shift the isobar on the weather map about 4 millibars nearer the coast (figure 9.2) and judge the wind that way.

The increase in speed is clearly greatest when the morning wind is in something like the same direction as the thermal component. The two then add together to give a stronger wind in the afternoon. An increase of 5 or 6 knots between 1100 and 1400 is fairly typical, followed of course by a decrease by the same amount as the sun goes down. This speed increase is of the same magnitude as the decrease caused by the diverging streamlines (figure 3.8), over the same coastal zone. So the net effect is to remove the area of slacker winds during the afternoon. Close to the coast a slight bend inshore is likely to persist.

Differences from the true sea breeze

The main differences between this thermally enhanced wind and the true sea breeze are:
• The morning wind does not go through the sequence of calm; light and directly onshore; veering

and increasing.
• The full speed benefit of the thermal enhancement is achieved only when the morning wind is in about the same direction as the thermal. If the morning wind is directly onshore, you can expect a small veer but little increase in speed.
• The change in direction is not as great; unless the morning wind is very weak and almost directly onshore. With stronger morning winds the afternoon wind direction will only be near that of the true sea breeze if the morning wind direction is near it to start with.
• The increase in speed is spread fairly uniformly over a coastal zone several kilometres wide. With the sea breeze the wind is clearly strongest near the shore, and decreases steadily as you sail out.
• The wind is not greatly influenced by the topography of the land. It blows whether or not there are hills or mountains, and does not bend into the valleys like the sea breeze.

QUADRANT 4

A gradient wind in quadrant 4 is a south-easterly on a south-facing coast, a north-westerly on a north facing coast, and so on. The pressure is then

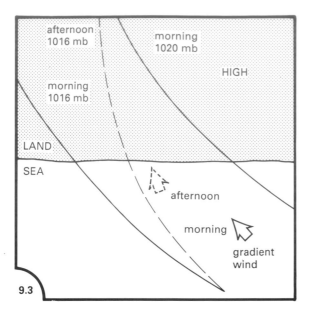

9.3

relatively high over the land (figure 9.3), and the reduction in pressure due to afternoon heating causes a reduction in pressure gradient and therefore in wind. The fall in pressure is the same as for the quadrant 3 situation, typically 2 to 5 millibars; the greater the rise in temperature the greater the fall in pressure.

Change in speed and direction

Again the change in the onshore wind depends on the relative strengths and directions of the gradient wind and the thermal component. Probably the easiest way to work it out is to refer to the weather map and reduce the pressure over the land while keeping it constant over the sea. In the typical high pressure situation of winds in quadrant 4 the initial pressure gradient is usually fairly slack, so the change due to heating is more noticeable. A decrease of 5 to 6 knots between mid-morning and mid-afternoon over a coastal zone several kilometres wide is fairly typical; the hotter the day the greater the change. If the morning wind is only a few knots to start with and blowing nearly parallel to the coast then it may be cancelled altogether as the land heats up. We are then into the 'no gradient wind situation' of Chapter 7 and the decks are cleared for a pure sea breeze.

On the Cote d'Azur the morning wind is frequently between east and east-south-east, and when, as often happens, it is about 6 to 10 knots it

dies away to not much more than a zephyr in the afternoon. If it is 5 knots or less it drops to calm by mid-afternoon and is followed by a moderate to fresh sea breeze blowing in from the south-west, arriving sometimes as late as 1700 local time.

Tactics

There are no clear-cut guides to finding the strongest wind in quadrant 3 and 4 situations on a sunny afternoon. In fact you can expect the wind to be relatively featureless within at least 5 km of the coast, without any noticeable structure; but sometimes decreasing fairly abruptly around 8 to 10 km out to sea.

If it is cloudy and the wind is fairly strong, heating of the land will be minimal and you should continue to look for the zones of slacker and stronger winds respectively as shown in figures 3.8 and 3.6.

As to wind direction, with a quadrant 3 wind you can expect a gradual change towards 15 degrees back from the coast with a slight bend inshore close to the shore. Note that the change will be gradual – not rapid to start with as with the sea breeze – and it may not stop swinging until mid-afternoon or until it has reached 15 degrees from the shoreline.

With a quadrant 4 wind the wind will veer as it dies. Do not expect a bend into the shore.

MARGINAL CASES

Gradient wind nearly parallel to the coast

In theory both the quadrant 1/3 and 2/4 boundaries need to be studied; but in reality you only meet the quadrant 1/3 situation – and you meet it quite often. The main questions to be answered are:
- whether or not there is a component of offshore wind which will support a sea breeze, and
- if there *is* an offshore component in the morning, whether it will last into the afternoon.

Small changes in the pressure pattern can easily tip the balance between an offshore and onshore wind. The change in pressure due to heating of the land is a change you can forecast for yourself merely by noting whether or not it is sunny.

If the gradient wind is less than about 10 knots and the day is hot a wind direction which is just inside quadrant 1 in the morning may change to quadrant 3. In this case the surface wind, initially alongshore and lighter near the shore, backs to what you would expect with the gradient parallel to the coast, i.e.

angled at 15 degrees onto the shore. The speed increases by 5 to 6 knots because of the increase in gradient, not because it is a sea breeze. There is no reason to expect the breeze to be either lighter or stronger near the shore than elsewhere.

If the gradient wind is blowing at more than about 15 knots heating of the land is unlikely to shift it out of quadrant 1, in which case you can expect figure 8.3 to apply.

'Tug of war'

Occasionally, when the day starts with a morning quadrant 1 gradient of only 3 or 4 knots you will find a genuine sea breeze developing onto the shore for an hour or so, then as heating changes the gradient the sea breeze turns into a characterless alongshore wind angled at about 15 degrees to the coast and not increasing above about 12 knots. A bend in the coast of a few degrees may tip the balance for or against a genuine sea breeze, creating something of a tug-of-war between the two types of wind.

This situation occurs off Barcelona, where a change in shore alignment from 245 degrees to 210 degrees (figure 3.9) makes marginal cases more frequent. Since it is impossible to predict in advance precisely how the light morning gradient will change during the day I devised the following simple on-the-water guidelines:

• Low cumulus or stratocumulus clouds continuing to move offshore and dissolve are evidence of an offshore gradient wind persisting; in which case expect a full sea breeze to develop, increasing to 20 knots inshore, rather less further out, and with the final direction about 20 degrees to the shoreline.

• Low clouds which become stationary mid-morning, or a sea breeze which starts, then falters and fails to increase over a period of about half an hour, both indicate a change to an alongshore gradient due to heating of the land; in which case expect the afternoon wind to settle down to about 10 to 12 knots, angled about 15 degrees to the shoreline with a slight bend inshore close to the coast but no other significant features.

10 Afternoon winds on lakes and peninsulas

The principles outlined in Chapters 7, 8 and 9 describing what happens when the land warms relative to the water can be applied to all coastlines and inland waters of any size in the Northern Hemisphere. If the afternoon is warm expect a sea or lake breeze, more wind or less wind, depending on whether the gradient wind is in quadrant 1 or 2, 3 or 4.

Some analysts trying to catalogue their observation of coastal breezes have sought to distinguish different sorts of sea breeze or they have regarded each venue as unique, requiring individual classification. They talk of local sea breezes and ocean breezes and suggest they behave differently in different places. But in fact the one critical factor on which everything else depends is the direction of the pressure gradient wind. In my experience there is just one sea breeze which is generated in the same way the world over. With the whole compass range of possible gradient wind directions and an even greater variety of coastline shapes there is scope for many sea breeze situations, but all of them are capable of being understood as outlined here.

The following examples should help you to appreciate the effect of the gradient wind in all cases. For specific case studies turn to Chapter 21.

A lake

We saw on page 36 that many lakes are too small to support a lake breeze onto all shores. With a gradient wind blowing across the lake there is a greater chance of finding a reasonable lake breeze because it develops onto one shore only, and will be preferentially supported from the area to the left of the breeze where the diverging streamlines encourage subsidence.

With a small lake, say less than 10 km across, the only thermal effect to look for – we looked at frictional effects on page 22 – is a light lake breeze on to the upwind shore, but it will be fitful because there is not enough water area to support it. The larger the lake, the more likely you are to find all the thermal effects at work on the various shores, depending on the angle of the gradient wind (figure 10,1).

A peninsula

In the first case (figure 10.2) there is no gradient wind: on a sunny day the breeze develops onto both the major shores, blowing towards the middle of the peninsula where a band of cumulus clouds may be seen. Once the two breezes meet they will start to die. The peninsula needs to be at least 100 km wide to sustain full-strength breezes onto both shores throughout the afternoon. Figure 10.3 shows how sea breezes move inland; the forward edge, often marked by towering cumulus clouds, is called a sea breeze front.

In the second case (figure 10.4) the gradient wind is either onshore or alongshore so no sea breeze can develop. There will be zones of lighter or stronger wind, and depending on the width of the peninsula these will be modified by afternoon heating. On a narrow peninsula, less than about 50 km wide, the wind component due to heating of the land will be too small to have a significant effect on the wind. The same goes for a small island.

The third case (figure 10.5) is ripe for a good quadrant 1 type sea breeze onto the downwind

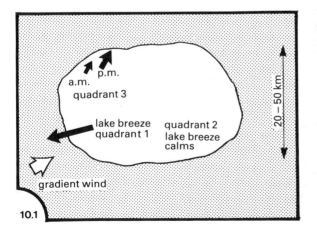

10.1

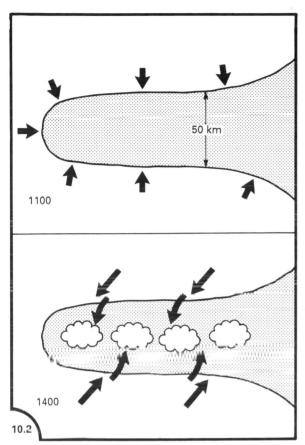

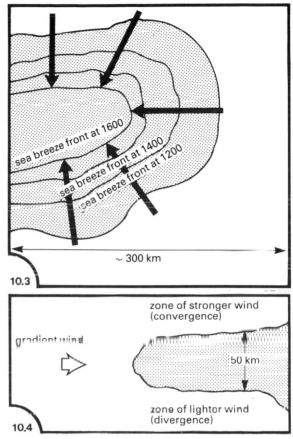

10.2

10.3

10.4

shore. 50 km is not quite wide enough to allow maximum strength to be reached, but a force 3 to 4 can be expected. However, do not be surprised if the breeze dies early, having moved inland at from 10 to 20 km per hour and reached the opposite shore of the peninsula.

The fourth peninsula situation (figure 10.6) is an interesting one. The breeze starts onto the end at B, a quadrant 1 situation, but as it veers and bends to the coastline it increases on the more southerly-facing coast, and dies away at B with some bending of the gradient wind likely around the corner.

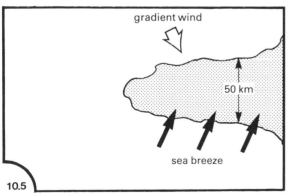

10.5

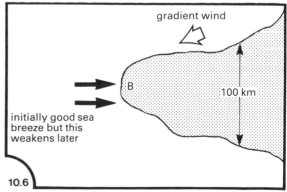

10.6

Above: towering cumulus developing over land as temperatures rise higher than the sea temperature and the sea breeze moves inland.

Spain

Winds around the Spanish peninsula in the summer half year are a good example of a quadrant 3 situation. For much of the time the weather map (figure 10.7) shows a shallow low-pressure area over the country, and each day the pressure falls some 3 to 5 millibars due to the heating of the land, recovering at night. The detailed shape of the isobars varies from day to day. It is often influenced by thunderstorms breaking out in late afternoon and continuing into the night, especially in late summer.

On average the morning wind is in quadrant 3: light southerly on the Mediterranean coast, light northerly on the Atlantic coast, and so on. Every afternoon the thermal vector parallel to the coast enhances the morning wind to give a wind typically in the range force 2 to 4. Fresh to strong sea breezes are rare because there is rarely an offshore component to the gradient wind.

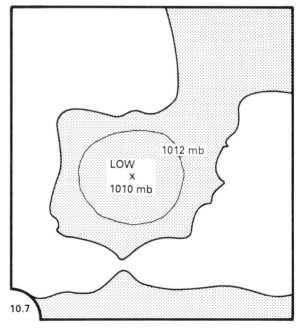

10.7

11 As the sun goes down

Inshore the three main things to consider are:
- The decay of the sea breeze.
- The change in gradient as the land cools.
- The onset of a land breeze.

The decay of the sea breeze

The sea breeze, which requires an offshore gradient wind in quadrants 1 or 2 (figure 8.1), will die fairly quickly in the evening, with a brief calm interval before the offshore gradient takes over again. If you can, check whether there has been any change in gradient wind since you last saw a weather chart. Your best on-the-spot guide will be the movement of any low cloud that may be around.

It is normal for the offshore wind to reappear first near the shore – within a mile or so – and then extend steadily seaward (figure 11.1). The stronger the gradient the quicker it returns. If the skies are clear the cooling of the land will mean a rapid decrease in wind over the land (see figure 2.6 and page 12), so do not stand in too close to the shore. The returning wind from the land will be weakening within about three miles downwind of the shore, and as it dies overland it will die close in until a land breeze materialises.

Change in gradient

If the gradient wind is in quadrants 3 and 4 the cooling of the land will remove the afternoon

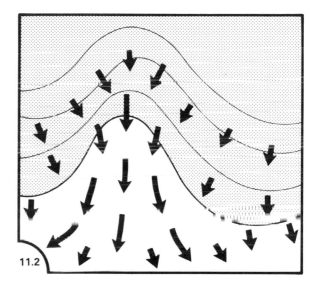

11.2

thermal vector and the gradient will revert to what it was earlier in the day. The quadrant 3 wind will become relatively light again within about 5 km of the coast, and the quadrant 4 wind will become that much stronger inshore.

The land breeze

The best way to visualize a land breeze is as a 'drainage' wind, flowing down hillsides, into valleys and out to sea rather like water (figure 11.2). On a

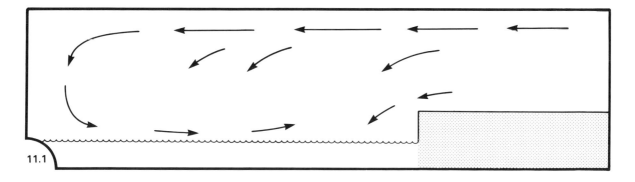

11.1

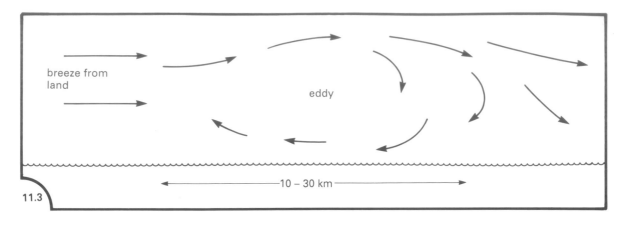

breeze from
land

eddy

10 – 30 km

11.3

clear night the land cools rapidly, and cools the air close to it. This cold air is relatively dense and so drains downwards following the contours of the land: the steeper the slope the stronger the breeze. On reaching the sea it spreads out fanwise and its momentum carries it a mile or two out to sea before it warms up and stops moving.

On coasts with relatively little high ground the land breeze is not particularly reliable. You have to stand in very close to benefit, and it tends to peter out in between valleys. Near mountainous country, on the other hand, land breezes can reach 30 knots or more and extend upwards of 50 km out to sea (see also Chapter 13). After blowing for a few hours the breeze is turned to the right by the influence of the Earth's rotation.

An offshore gradient wind may be enhanced by a land breeze, particularly downwind from valleys, where instead of the wind dying away inshore at night it keeps going.

When the gradient wind is onshore the development of the land breeze depends on the strength of the gradient and whether there is coastal convergence or divergence (figures 3.6 and 3.8). With a light wind and coastal divergence you should expect to find a shallow land breeze close to the shore beneath the onshore wind, especially near a valley. With an onshore wind of force 4 or more and coastal convergence, only a mountainous coast will produce a land breeze.

Offshore
Offshore you should look for the following:
• Under a low cloud there may be a gradual increase in wind by anything from 1 to 6 knots as the top of the cloud cools (see page 13). You will have to judge for yourself whether there is high cloud present to reduce the cooling of the low cloud.
• If there are large cumulus or cumulonimbus clouds around there is an increased likelihood of showers or thunderstorms as the cloud tops cool. To avoid a storm try to leave it to port (see page 62), but this advice does not apply in the Doldrums, where the storms move westwards most of the time, and in any case you will probably be looking to the storm to provide some wind.
• If the breeze is offshore and you are within 200 km or so of the coast, there will probably be a temporary reversal in wind as dying remnants of the previous afternoon's sea breeze roll away from the coast (figure 11.3). A typical sea breeze eddy moves out from the land at something like two-thirds of the component of wind speed perpendicular to the coast; so you can make a rough estimate of its arrival time. Assume that the sea breeze has reached 50 km offshore at about 1700hrs.

12 Afternoon and evening winds in the Southern Hemisphere

Let us now consider the features described in Chapters 7 to 11 with reference to the Southern Hemisphere. Again, as we saw in Chapter 6, the arguments concerning the influences of the unequal heating and cooling of land and water by day and night are virtually identical. The relevant diagrams are largely mirror images of those applying to the Northern Hemisphere.

The pure sea breeze – no gradient wind
The sea breeze develops as a growing closed circulation as shown in Figure 7.1, with the onshore flow being supplied from air moving seawards at a higher level and subsiding over the colder water. Its characteristics and signs are as described in Chapter 7 except that instead of turning to the right it turns to the left, whichever direction the coast faces; the final direction being approximately 20 degrees seaward of the shoreline. All the figures illustrating the initial

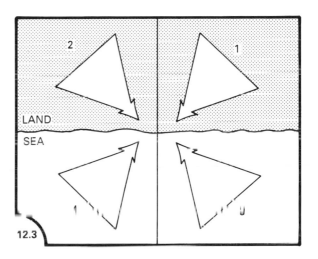

12.3

stages of the breeze apply: 7.2, 7.3, 7.5, and 7.7. But for the later stages figure 12.1 replaces 7.4, and figure 12.2 replaces 7.8.

Sea breeze with gradient wind blowing
As in the Northern Hemisphere, the sea breeze is critically dependent on the presence of an offshore component to the gradient wind. The Southern Hemisphere equivalent to 'quadrant 1' are wind directions between east and south on a west-facing shore, between south and west on a north-facing shore, and so on (figure 12.3). These are the gradient wind directions for the best sea breezes

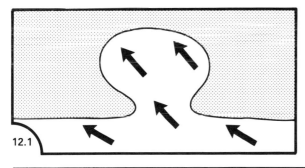

12.1

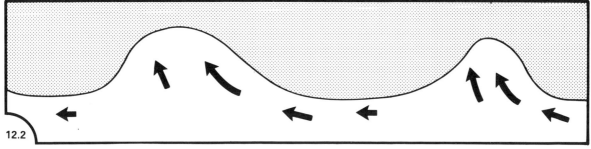

12.2

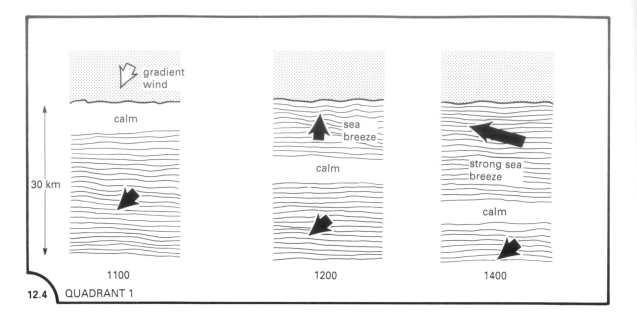

12.4 QUADRANT 1

which develop as illustrated in figure 12.4 – or 12.5 if the initial surface wind direction is nearly parallel to the coast. In cross-section figure 8.5 still applies.

When the gradient wind is in quadrant 2 (figure 12.3) there is a tendency for the land and sea winds near the coast to converge, so the breeze starts seaward of the coast as shown in figure 12.6 and we have two calm zones (cross-section figure 8.6), one moving seawards and the other towards the shore. The behaviour and speed of movement of the calm zones is as described on page 42.

Afternoon winds when the gradient wind is onshore

Although the wind is onshore it does not have the characteristics of the genuine sea breeze described above. Its behaviour is distinctly different in both speed and direction. Splitting the range of directions into quadrants 3 and 4 (figure 12.6) makes it easier to distinguish between the coastal divergence situation (land on right when standing back to the wind) and the coastal convergence situation (land on left when standing back to the wind).

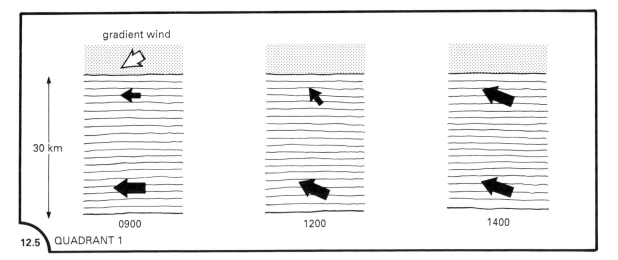

12.5 QUADRANT 1

When the gradient wind is in Quadrant 3 the pressure is relatively low over the land. Afternoon heating reduces it still further so that:
- The strength increases: ranging from an additional 5 or 6 knots if the initial wind direction is 15 degrees veered from the coast, to virtually zero if the wind is directly onshore.
- The direction bends towards a line 15 degrees veered from the coast, by an amount depending on the strength of the gradient wind relative to the thermal enhancement. A light morning wind will be shifted more than a strong one.

When the gradient wind is in quadrant 4 the pressure is relatively high over the land and is reduced by afternoon heating so that:
- The strength decreases: the more it is aligned to the shore the greater the decrease.
- The direction veers – the lighter the morning wind the greater the veer.
- If the gradient dies completely a late sea breeze follows.

The *'Fremantle Doctor'* saga of the 1986/7 America's Cup series provides a good example of the difference between a genuine sea breeze and an onshore gradient wind. Popular weather opinion was that the Fremantle Doctor was notably reliable, guaranteed to blow on at least 90 per cent of afternoons, and invariably at force 6. In the event Force 6 was experienced on less than half the occasions; the more frequent 12 to 15 knots was described as 'unusual'.

In the event it proved possible on most mornings to predict whether a force 4 or force 6 would materialise simply by reference to the gradient wind. A south-easterly (quadrant 1) would be followed by a Fremantle Doctor, the genuine sea breeze, which increased to force 6 by mid-afternoon. An onshore gradient, typically between south-south-west and south-west (quadrant 3) would increase by a mere 6 or 7 knots to force 4. There were also subtle and predictable differences in the final direction for the same reason.

As the sun goes down
The decay of the sea breeze, the change in gradient as the land cools, and the onset of the land breeze all follow the pattern described in Chapter 11.

The offshore wind reappears first near the shore (quadrant 1 and 2 situations) subsequently extending steadily seawards, often with a cut-off and dying sea breeze eddy (figure 11.3) travelling seawards on the offshore wind for up to 12 hours or so before finally disappearing.

With a gradient wind in quadrants 3 and 4 the gradient reverts to what it was – unless of course larger-scale changes are in train. A nearshore wind maximum returns in the quadrant 4 case, and a nearshore minimum in quadrant 3.

The land breeze, being a drainage wind that flows down slopes and out to sea rather like water, shows the same characteristics in both hemispheres. But if it has been blowing for a few hours it starts to turn to the left under the influence of the Earth's rotation.

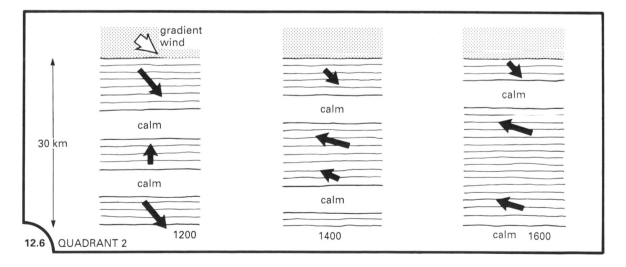

12.6 QUADRANT 2

13 Mountain and valley winds, gravity waves and billows

In mountainous areas the pressure gradient wind will either be bent to blow along the valleys, if it is aligned somewhere near that direction; or else it will blow across the tops of the mountains leaving only eddies in the valleys, similar to those of figure 13.4.

Frequently there is some form of cold air drainage wind to be found among mountains: relatively dense cold air flowing downhill and accumulating in valleys in the same way that water flows down towards the sea. To understand how these winds blow, remember that:

● Cold air takes the easiest and most obvious route down towards the sea – predictable from a contour map of the area.

● If there is a choice of equally likely routes the pressure gradient determines which.

Figure 13.1 is an example of these points. Cold air draining down valley A can continue down valley B or valley C. Because of the direction of the pressure gradient there is a westerly component to the gradient wind and the cold air will drain down valley C.

There are two main sources of cold air, either of which can result in surface drainage winds of up to 40 knots or more; the speed depending on how much cold air is available and the height, slope and shape of the mountains and valleys.

Air cooled at night by cold ground under a clear sky

The relatively dense cooled air flows downhill and accumulates in the valleys. If it meets an obstruction it will pile up until it eventually breaks through like water breaking through a dam. A sudden gush of wind follows, and will last a short or long time depending on how much air has piled up. Strong and sudden valley breezes of this type are frequently experienced between early morning and shortly after sunrise. They may last only half an hour or so.

Cold air from behind a cold front This gives a much steadier and more persistent breeze which often achieves local fame with its own name.

When a cold front reaches a mountain barrier the cold air being relatively dense piles up against the barrier until it finds a valley route down to the sea. In the case of the Alps, one to two days after a cold front has reached the mountains the cold air is found escaping south down the main valleys. The Rhone valley is one route south and the local wind is called

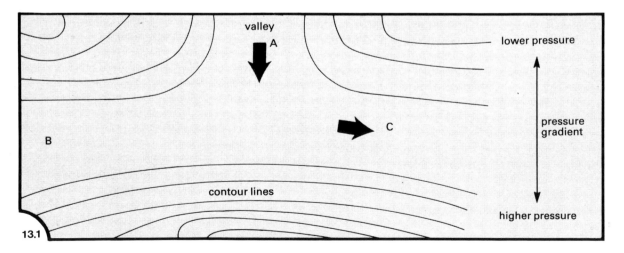

13.1

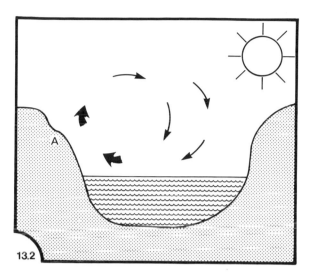

13.2

the Mistral. Normally there is enough cold air piled up against the mountains to keep the Mistral going for several days.

Breezes on steep-sided lakes
The development of lake breezes is discussed in Chapter 7. In mountainous regions there are other factors affecting the wind.

No gradient wind, some sunshine, lake breeze develops A lake breeze will develop onto the sunny hillside, and more often than not will form a closed circulation, the strongest winds being close to the sunny shore (A in figure 13.2). The wind may veer as the sun moves round and shines onto other sides of the lake.

Lake in a valley, gradient wind blowing along line of valley The surface wind will blow approximately in the direction of the gradient wind, i.e. guided by the line of the valley, but its strength will depend on the air stability within the valley, the origin of this air and whether the valley is closed or open (figure 13.3).

   If the valley provides a clear route through a mountain range the wind will funnel strongly along the valley, particularly when the air is stable and therefore reluctant to rise over the mountains.

Lake in a valley, gradient wind blowing across the valley The airflow is likely to separate and the steeper the edge the more readily it separates. The eddy forms on the side of the valley towards the gradient wind. The steeper the side, the larger the eddy (A and B in figure 13.4).

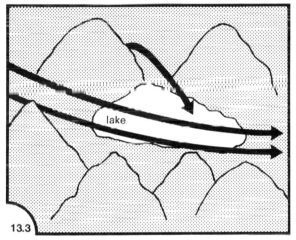

13.3

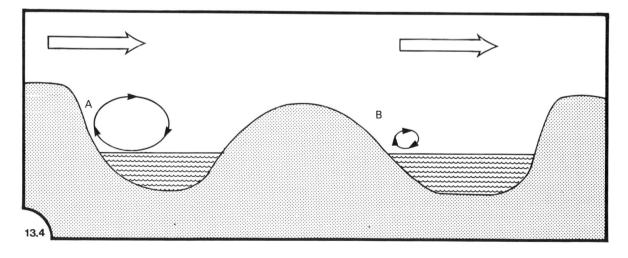

13.4

GRAVITY WAVES

The term 'gravity waves' is used by meteorologists to embrace several wind phenomena, some of which have already been described. A squall line sweeping out from a raining cloud (Chapter 14) is a gravity wave: cooled and relatively heavy air falling under gravity, spreading outwards and hugging the ground because it cannot fall any further. So is a land breeze or drainage wind (Chapter 11): cold heavy air sliding down a hillside under gravity. I have introduced the term here because I want to add another and somewhat rarer event to the catalogue – a gravity wave experienced occasionally behind a cold front, sometimes called a cold surge.

I met one of these during the 1-ton World Championships at Kiel in June 1991. A cold front had crossed from the north and the wind had veered to north-westerly force 3 to 4 as forecast. An hour or so after the veer the wind suddenly increased to force 6 for about 20 minutes, with vicious cold gusts and a further veer of some 40 to 50 degrees, accompanied by a rather ragged roll of low cloud. Somewhat higher cloud, thin stratocumulus at about 1500 metres, showed no response to what was going on below and continued to move slowly southwards.

Taking all the evidence together this was a 'lump' of very cold air that had probably 'fallen off' the Norwegian mountains, rushing southwards and hugging the ground because it was dense and heavy. There was no sign of it at 1500 metres up.

Maybe up to 20 per cent of cold fronts in continental areas are followed within a few hours by some sort of gravity wave, so be prepared. Over and downwind from oceans a more clearly defined multiple cold front is more likely, with a relatively minor cold front following behind the main one an hour or two later.

Waves and billows

If you flew over a large area of low cloud covering the sea you might see a series of regular undulations – waves – in the cloud top, not unlike a long, low sea swell. These are evidence of a wave motion in the air, similar to the effect downwind of a cliff (figure 3.11). Meteorologists call them Kelvin-Helmholtz waves. Every few hundred waves you might see one of them breaking, just like a sea wave, with a ragged crest in the cloud and a suggestion of turbulence. This is a billow.

Beneath the cloud and down near the sea surface (figure 13.5) you would find that the crests and troughs in the cloud top corresponded to minima and maxima in the wind, with as much as 2 or 3 knots difference between them, similar to the banding in the wind described on page 23. The breaking wave (or billow) would be producing turbulence right down to the sea surface with the speed and direction fluctuating wildly for 2 or 3 minutes – typically between 1 and 12 knots in an otherwise 6 to 8 knot wind. Such a billow coming apparently out of nowhere can be quite unnerving until you realise what it is.

These waves form only in stable air; they were observed, for example, on the old America's Cup course at Newport Rhode Island. But by far the most commonly experienced case of billows is inflight turbulence, often in clear air, but sometimes revealed by billow clouds which can be seen from the window of the aircraft or from the ground. The regular pattern of tufts in the cirrus or cirrostratus look just like a series of breaking sea waves.

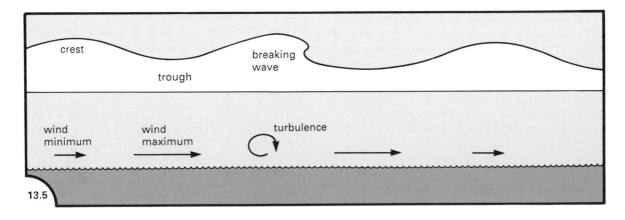

crest

trough

breaking
wave

wind
minimum

wind
maximum

turbulence

13.5

14 The message of the clouds

Clouds reveal a great variety of events in the atmosphere, some of them involving changes in the wind. On pictures taken from satellites above the Earth the clouds act as a dye in the air, mapping out the large-scale weather systems. Particularly noticeable are the depressions with their attendant troughs and fronts. They also suggest many and varied smaller-scale wind movements down to the limits of resolution of the pictures – about 6 kilometres.

Looked at from below, the clouds are just as meaningful but their message relates to events on a much smaller scale, a mere few hundred metres or so. Cumulus clouds, for instance, tell of pockets of rising air which are replaced by air moving downward in between the clouds. Occasionally there may be no wind except for air moving towards a large cumulus cloud from all directions around it. In fact every cloud has a message of some sort, though not necessarily about the wind. The sailor needs to recognise features of the clouds which relate to the character of the wind, or which indicate that there may be a change in the wind during the period of a race.

Many books about the weather concentrate on the large-scale systems, the depressions and anticyclones, and a great deal is written about fronts and the changes in wind that go with them. These are very important for anyone contemplating an ocean race, but not very significant for a dinghy sailor about to race for three to four hours on an Olympic course.

I have no doubt however that knowledge of the clouds can help win races. I will not say much about the higher clouds, because their message is normally about events far aloft or several hours ahead. Instead I want to concentrate on evidence of wind changes from minutes to two or three hours ahead, and also to try to rule out signs which are unimportant or capable of misleading. Let us first consider a few observations from a layman's point of view.

Black and white clouds
The colour of a cloud depends on how it is illuminated. If the sun is shining on it, it will appear white; if the sun is behind it, it will appear dark. If it is illuminated at a glancing angle when the sun is rising or setting, it will be beautifully coloured.

The colour will change as the cloud moves across the sky or as the sun changes altitude. This change in colour is of no consequence where the wind is concerned. Similarly a sailor's impression of a layer of haze over the land will also change as the angle of the sun changes and must not be interpreted as indicating a change of wind.

Bent clouds
When cumulus clouds appear bent it means that the tops are moving faster than their bases owing to a marked increase in wind speed with height. These clouds suggest a greater than normal difference in speed and direction between gusts and lulls at the surface.

Flat clouds
Flat clouds are characteristic of stable air. They often possess some shape or structure but this is usually due to warming or cooling of the top of the cloud and must not be interpreted in terms of any wind pattern at the surface. However a large and distinctive feature appearing in a layer of cloud may have significance.

Lumpy clouds
Lumpy or cumulus clouds are characteristic of unstable air. They are found most frequently over land in the afternoon when the temperature is at a maximum, when pockets of air heated at the ground rise until the cooling due to expansion brings their temperature back to that of the surrounding air.

Look for the moment at a single cumulus cloud (figure 14.1). If it is stationary, that is if there is no gradient wind, air will rise from the heated ground into the cloud to be replaced by air moving down

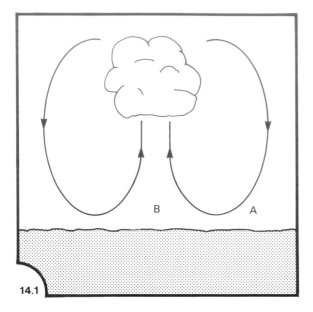

14.1

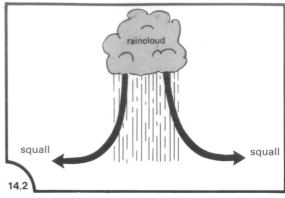

14.2

(subsiding) around the outside of the cloud, creating a very simple circulation pattern. The wind strength in the inflow area is indicated by the size of the cloud; for a small cloud, say 100 metres across and 300 metres in vertical extent, it will be less than a knot, but for a towering cumulus cloud of the order of 500 metres across and up to 5000 metres vertically it may be 15 or more knots.

In practice there is usually some pressure gradient wind, and the gentle convergence of air into a small cloud is only a very minor detail superimposed on the main wind. However, even with a small cumulus cloud there is likely to be a detectable difference in the wind between point A in figure 14.1 where the wind is strongest and most veered, and point B where the wind is lightest and most backed.

Raining clouds

So far we have considered fair-weather clouds, or at least clouds where there is no sign of any rain falling. Rain makes a fundamental difference to the wind characteristics of clouds. The main reason for this is that the first rain to fall out of the base of the cloud evaporates into the air beneath and cools it, often by several degrees. This cooled air descends and the more it is cooled the more rapidly it descends. Thus instead of air rising into a cloud we have not only rain falling out but air as well.

The drier the air beneath the cloud the more it is capable of being cooled by evaporation, and so long as there is enough rain coming out of the cloud the colder the air becomes. The cooled air will literally drop out from beneath the cloud with the rain and spread out in all directions at the surface. Thus the light wind moving in towards the cloud suddenly becomes a squall rushing out and away from it (figure 14.2).

There is always plenty of visual evidence of this change. You can see the rain falling, often grey streaks below the cloud, sometimes a dramatic arch of black cloud spreading out from the cloud. The squall is necessarily short-lived because there is only a limited amount of air below the cloud to be cooled by evaporation of the rain into it. Once the squall has passed the rain usually continues for a while, some 10 to 20 minutes for a typical shower cloud before it is exhausted. The wind coming out of the cloud will gradually die away with the rain.

Left: cumulus clouds forming over cooling towers. Opposite, top: in front of the sun a cloud appears dark. This one is not as threatening as it looks. Below: bent cumulus cloud showing wind increasing with height.

Usually there is a pressure gradient wind, but often the squall from a reasonably sized shower cloud will temporarily override the pressure gradient wind, and will augment it where they are both in the same direction.

Tactics

If you see a cloud raining, or about to rain, out to either side of the course, head for it. You will be lifted as you go across, and can then tack as the squall hits you and be lifted towards the mark (figure 14.3). But don't head for a non-raining cloud – the effect is opposite and you will lose ground.

Thunderstorms

The larger shower clouds keep going for longer and develop a complex structure, with rain falling from part of the cloud while air continues to be drawn up into another part. The name 'cumulonimbus' is sometimes reserved for these big clouds.

A small thunderstorm (one or two claps) is likely to be very similar to a passing heavy shower, the pressure gradient wind being temporarily masked by the squall coming out of the cloud.

A large thunderstorm cumulonimbus may last for an hour or more, sometimes three or four hours. The larger the thunderstorm the more the local pressure pattern and winds for some distance around

are controlled by it. The very largest storms, known in the trade as 'severe storms', are self-generating and steered by the winds high in the atmosphere. The majority of smaller storms move to the right of the surface wind (looking downwind). So if you want to avoid the storm, set a course to leave it to port (Northern Hemisphere). If you want more wind and need the shift from the storm use the tactics described above for a raining cloud.

Safety A tall mast, just like a tree or any other free-standing object, will tend to be a focal point for a lightning discharge to earth, so it is important to ensure that the conducting route (metal) through to the water is continuous. If the mast is stepped in wood or glassfibre and the shroud plates are fixed into wood or glassfibre with no metal components extending below the waterline, a lightning strike is likely to result in a hole burnt through the hull. Helmsmen and crew are safe sitting well aft and not holding onto the shrouds.

Lines or bands of high cloud

I have already mentioned the most commonly-discussed cloud bands: the large-scale fronts and troughs which feature on the weather map and are revealed in satellite pictures. The major windshifts associated with them can rarely be pinpointed with sufficient accuracy to be of use when beating to windward on an Olympic course. All you can hope to apply is the knowledge that the wind backs and increases ahead of a trough or front, and if you are racing on a day with increasing cloud and falling pressure this can be very useful.

More detailed knowledge of fronts and troughs comes into its own in an offshore race and is considered in *Weather at Sea* in this series. But before moving on to discuss the message of bands of low cloud there is one high cloud sign which can prove useful.

Occasionally a clear-cut cloud edge is seen extending right across the sky, with blue sky or thin cirrus cloud one side and thicker-looking high-level and middle-level cloud the other side. If the cloud band is stationary it is likely that there will be no change in the gradient wind for several hours. But if the band is moving so that the cloud is increasing and thickening, it is a sure sign of an increasing and backing wind. The stronger the high-level winds revealed by the cloud band the greater the change to come.

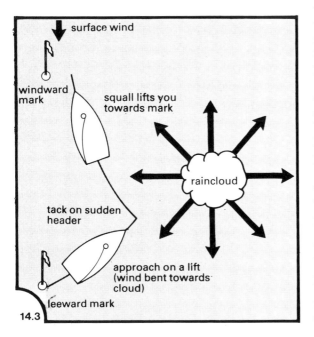

surface wind

windward mark

squall lifts you towards mark

raincloud

tack on sudden header

approach on a lift (wind bent towards cloud)

leeward mark

14.3

Top: stratocumulus cloud has a
characteristic roll or banded structure.
Centre: an advancing line of
stratocumulus clouds indicates an
approaching windshift. Bottom: fair
weather cumulus clouds.

Top: cumulonimbus. Typical heavy shower cloud. Centre: line of cumulus clouds indicating marked windshift. Bottom: cloud increasing ahead of an advancing trough of low pressure.

Lines of low cloud – moving

Minor troughs Whereas it is almost impossible to anticipate the precise time of the change of wind associated with a weather feature as large as a front or trough of low pressure, the change accompanying a line of low cloud is almost directly beneath the line of cloud. When you see it coming you can prepare for its arrival, and judge it accurately enough to use the change to advantage on a beat or run. It is often useful to think of an advancing line of low cloud as a smaller replica of the larger-scale 'weather map' system: a very minor trough in the atmosphere giving a small (and perhaps temporary) veer in wind direction as it goes by (figure 14.4), probably preceded by a back of 2 or 3 degrees.

A good example are the lines of sometimes towering cumulus clouds which are frequently met in unstable airstreams following a cold front. They can be seen approaching, and the windshift, often gusty, may be anticipated to within a few minutes. If rain is falling out of the individual towering cumulus clouds you can expect a more dramatic change with a squall coming out of the cloud (figure 14.2, 14.3) before the wind settles down to the new, more veered direction. You can either steer to avoid the squall, or use it.

A new wind There are occasions when a line of low cloud approaches from a direction very different from the wind you are sailing in. You may have next to no wind, or you may be near the coast in an old land breeze or a weak sea breeze. It is then particularly important to recognise that the line of cloud moving towards you is the sign of a new gradient wind arriving. Its direction and speed of advance will be the direction and speed of the new gradient wind, with the wind on the water 15 degrees back.

The approach of a bank of fog sometimes marks the arrival of the sea breeze. At other times it may herald less wind, because fog is a feature of very stable air where vertical mixing is inhibited and the effect of friction becomes more pronounced. If the wind is light to start with it may be calm in the fog.

Cloud streets This is the name given to the regularly spaced lines of cumulus clouds which are often found over the open sea. They are associated with a pattern in the vertical movement of air which is like the horizontal roll illustrated in figure 4.1. The best examples are found in the trade winds where they

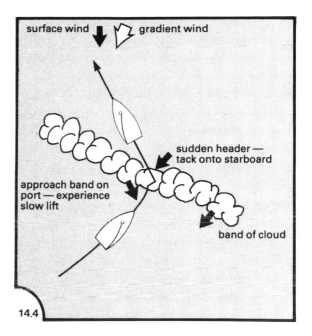

surface wind   gradient wind

sudden header — tack onto starboard

approach band on port — experience slow lift

band of cloud

14.4

extend for many hundreds of kilometres. The surface winds are equally disturbed or uneven, with relatively backed and lighter winds beneath the clouds and veered and stronger winds in the intervening clear lanes (figure 14.5).

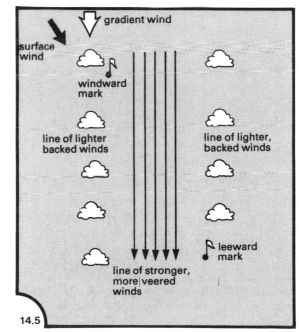

gradient wind

surface wind

windward mark

line of lighter backed winds

line of lighter, backed winds

line of stronger, more veered winds

leeward mark

14.5

Above: a well-marked cloud street lying along the wind direction.

The differences are not great, only a few degrees, but are sufficiently regular to be worth using. When beating through the streets you will quickly discover the position of the cloud lines relative to the shifts and anticipate your tack accordingly. When reaching you will go through the gusts and lulls quite quickly so constant sail trim will be needed. On the run, gybe on the shifts to keep the wind most abeam.

Lines of low cloud – stationary
Stationary lines of cloud are often found in the following situations:
● With an onshore wind when cloud forms as the air rises over coastal hills.
● When standing waves have formed in the wind downwind of a cliff or hill (see figure 3.11).
● When the wind is blowing nearly parallel to the coast and the land wind and sea wind are converging (see figure 3.6).
● When adjacent areas of warm and cold water cause local convergence of airstreams (see figure 4.3).
● When cumulus clouds generated over a particular hot spot on land are carried downwind, forming a single cloud street.

The wind patterns in respect of the first four situations are discussed in the respective chapters. The stationary cloud street is likely to have a distinctive wind pattern over the water, with a lighter, backed wind under the cloud street and a stronger, veered wind either side, so long as the water is not too cold. In stable conditions with the sea cold relative to the air, the cumulus street from the land may not influence the wind on the water.

There are very many variations on the theme of lines and bands of cloud, and it is important to emphasise that the atmosphere is never completely uniform over an area. There are always variations and it is not always easy to distinguish between those lines of cloud that suggest a wind change at the surface and those that do not.

Fog
Fog forms over the sea when warm moist air blows over relatively cold water, the water cooling the air to below its dewpoint (the temperature below which condensation occurs). In winter and spring the sea is coldest inshore so fog forms more frequently along the coast than out to sea. In summer and autumn the sea is coldest away from the shore so fog forms more frequently out to sea. Since sea temperature normally varies from place to place there are likely to be variations also in the extent of sea fog.

Sometimes fog which has formed over the land on a clear night drifts out seawards from the coast, but it does not usually go far before dispersing and rarely more than 5 kilometres from the shore. What is more, as soon as it hits the sea, it starts clearing near the surface and by the time it is a hundred metres offshore it is usually clear to mast height.

In fog you should look for the following wind characteristics of stable air:
● Strong vertical shear (pages 12 and 79). The sails should be set with plenty of twist.
● Marked banding in the wind. This means no short period changes (gusts and lulls) but marked, though relatively gradual, windshifts on moving from one band to another.

15 Obstacles in the wind

An Olympic course will normally be sited well away from any obstacles which might upset the wind. Regattas on inland waters, however, can rarely be held in such ideal conditions, and river sailors in particular have to live with obstacles to the wind. So it is worth summarising the behaviour of the wind downwind of various sorts of barrier. This has a spin-off for the open-water Olympic course sailor who may well be faced with a barrier of larger boats ahead of him as he starts ten minutes behind another class.

There are many types and densities of barriers: buildings, trees, forests, walls, fences, boats, poles; some short, some tall, and so on, but their influence on the wind is a function primarily of the height and average density of the barrier. Density might be loosely defined as the amount of daylight that a barrier lets through. Thus a brick wall has a density of 100 per cent, a well-spaced row of trees a density of 30 per cent, etc. As a general rule, whatever the density of the barrier you need to go approximately 30 times the height of the barrier downwind before you are clear of its influence. For river sailors this is virtually impossible, but all is not lost for there are a few simple though not obvious guidelines as to where the best wind is likely to be.

Figure 15.1 is taken from a study of winds downwind of barriers conducted by R W Gloyne of

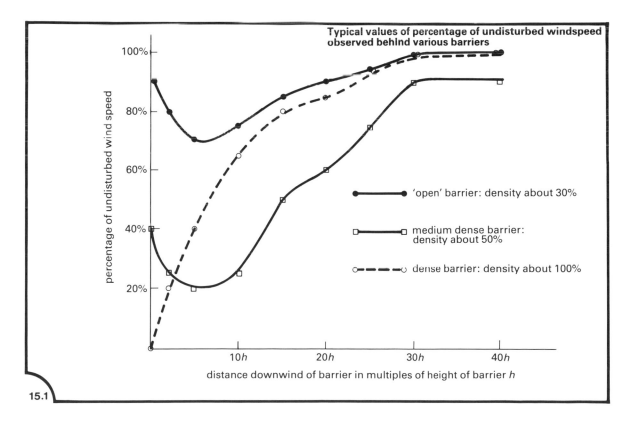

Typical values of percentage of undisturbed windspeed observed behind various barriers

● 'open' barrier: density about 30%

□ medium dense barrier: density about 50%

○ dense barrier: density about 100%

percentage of undisturbed wind speed

distance downwind of barrier in multiples of height of barrier *h*

15.1

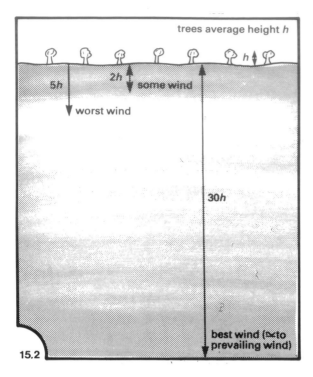

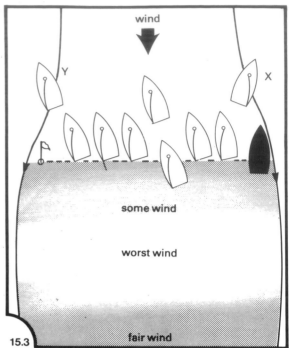

the UK Meteorological Office some years ago. It shows in particular that:

• For all but the more solid barriers there is a zone of lowest wind speed about 5 times the height of the barrier downwind from it. Figure 15.2 shows where the 'worst wind' area would be downwind from a line of trees.

• A medium-dense barrier is a much more effective obstacle to the wind than a dense one such as a brick wall or a thick hedge.

• For most barriers other than the medium-dense variety the wind recovers to 75 per cent of its average speed at a distance of roughly 10 times the height of the barrier downwind.

A massed start of a hundred or so boats could be described as a medium-dense barrier and is likely to disturb the wind for a distance up to 30 or 40 times its height downwind, i.e. up to 300 metres away. In figure 15.3 note that the fleet starting not only interferes with the wind, but causes it to bend around the edges. Thus boat X (on port) and Y (on starboard) both experience a lift.

Figure 15.4 points up the dangers of approaching the windward mark on port tack if you are fairly well down the fleet. The boats already on the reach will form a medium-dense barrier to the wind in which it will be almost impossible to sail.

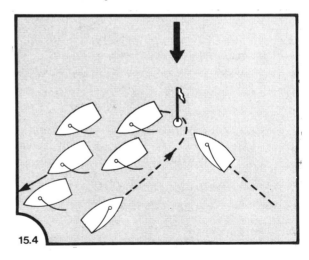

16 Currents

Water is normally moving in one direction or another for some reason, and a movement of as little as one or two tenths of a knot may be important to the racer. If the current is uniform over the racing area and constant throughout the race it does not benefit one helmsman over another. But if the current changes across the course or during the race you can take advantage of it.

For any particular place the pattern of ocean currents may be learned from the pilot for the area and the tidal streams can be worked out from the appropriate tidal atlas or nautical almanac. I want to consider here the variation from what is given in the pilot or almanac. Variations can crop up for four reasons:
- Interaction with the coast or islands.
- Variations in depth.
- The wind.
- Variations in temperature and salinity, including proximity to rivers.

Interaction with the coast or islands
You have only to watch a river to see how easily eddies form in a bay or inlet, downstream from an obstruction or at the edge of a particularly fast section of the flow. Some remain in the same place for long periods, others break away and move downstream.

Spotting eddies at sea is often a matter of commonsense coupled with observation. If a current is flowing past a bay or inlet it is very likely that an eddy will form, the details of the position and circulation depending upon the shape of the coastline and the depth of the water near the shore (figure 16.1).

Variations in depth
The current slows down (because of friction) as it passes over shallows or near the shore. But if the shallows extend right across a channel the current speeds up because the water has no alternative route (figure 16.2).

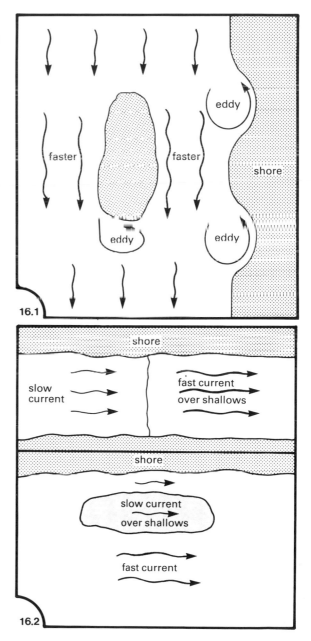

The wind

The effect of the wind is most marked when the surface water is relatively warm or fresh, or both. The surface layer is then stable and does not mix with the deeper water. In this situation a wind will drive the surface water downwind independently of the deeper water. A wind of 10 knots blowing over a surface layer of warm water about 1 metre deep will accelerate it to a speed of a knot or more within about 10 hours. This happened at the 1968 Olympic Yachting events in Acapulco: it was christened 'Acapulco's slippery sea'. We also observed in Acapulco that even if the wind died away the water would continue to move for a day or more. The direction of movement of a wind-driven current is initially directly downwind but due to the Earth's rotation there is a swing to the right (looking upwind) in the Northern Hemisphere and to the left in the Southern Hemisphere. The maximum swing will be 80 degrees over a period of 24 hours in mid-latitudes, though near the coast the swing will be constrained by the shore. In low latitudes the rate of swing is much slower.

Another wind effect is found in enclosed waters. Strong winds blowing for periods of a day or more pile the water up at the downwind end of the enclosure. The water movement is barely noticeable during the strong wind, but if the wind suddenly drops a significant current is likely as the water returns to its original level (figure 16.3). The time it takes for the water to return will depend on the subsequent wind and the size of the area of water. We observed a return flow at Kiel after periods of strong south-westerly winds during the pre-Olympic Kiel Week regattas. Here the water level took about 24 hours to return to normal when the wind died away.

If the water is strongly stratified the return flow when the wind drops may take place through a bottom current rather than a surface one. I observed this during a pre-Olympic regatta at Kingston, Lake Ontario, when cold bottom water suddenly appeared as a strong wind died away. There was little horizontal current.

Rivers

Considerable variation is found in surface currents near river mouths, and what happens often depends on the temperature of the river water. If its temperature is the same or higher than the sea temperature it will stay on top of the sea water unless the wind is strong enough to mix it mechanically. A top layer of fresh and perhaps warm water will behave as a slippery layer and will be driven by the wind independently of the water below (figure 16.4). The slippery sea at Acapulco was partly a consequence of a river outflow some 80 kilometres down the coast. If the river water is much colder than the sea temperature, as in winter and early spring around the coasts of Europe and western North America, it will sink rapidly and will not influence local currents except very close to the river mouth.

Near coasts, particularly estuaries, it is not unusual to find significantly different currents in adjacent areas of warm and cold water, the boundary being marked by a colour change and sometimes a band of pollution. Do not forget the influence on the wind of the change in water temperature described on page 24.

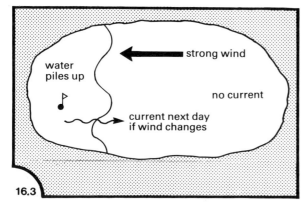

16.3

water piles up

strong wind

no current

current next day if wind changes

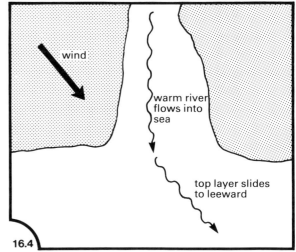

16.4

wind

warm river flows into sea

top layer slides to leeward

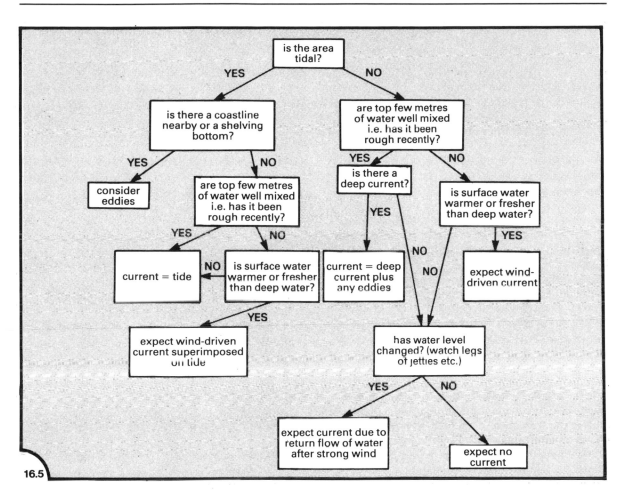

16.5

Observing the current

To measure the surface current you need firstly a fixed point and secondly some object which floats in the water, is easy to see and is not moved significantly by the wind.

Any buoy or lobster pot will do for the fixed point. The best and simplest float is a pole, one to one-and-a-half metres long, weighted with lead or rock at one end so that it floats vertically with not more than a few centimetres visible above the water. This top bit should be painted in a bright colour. Such a float will show the average current through the depth of water in which your boat sails.

Drop the float alongside the fixed point and note the distance and direction it moves over a period of a minute or two. If you haven't a pole handy, something like an apple core which floats mainly

below the surface of the water will give a good idea of the current on most occasions. But be cautious how you use the information on a sunny afternoon with a fairly smooth sea, because the water in the top few centimetres is likely to be 2° or 3°C warmer than below, and the top few centimetres may be sliding downwind while the water only to 6 to 7 centimetres further down is stationary.

It is worth measuring the temperature of the surface water if possible. Any thermometer is suitable though some are easier to use than others. A swim will often reveal temperature variations of 2° or 3°C; the body is very sensitive to these sorts of differences. And you can swim with the thermometer in your hand or between your toes!

To predict the current during a race, ask yourself the questions in figure 16.5.

17 Waves

It is customary to classify waves as two types: wind waves which are produced locally by the wind blowing at the time, and swell waves which are generated by the wind somewhere else. The 'somewhere else' can be thousands of miles away.

The height and distance apart of waves depends upon:
- The strength of the wind.
- The length of time it has been blowing.
- The fetch, which is the distance the wind has been blowing over the water.
- The depth of the water.
- In the case of swell, the distance the waves have travelled.

Wind waves
Locally produced wind waves are generated very quickly, within an hour or so, and provided the wind is steady and the fetch of sufficient distance, the longer it blows the longer the wavelength. The height achieved depends on the wind strength, and up to a certain limiting distance it increases with fetch. So, for instance, a wind of 10 knots blowing over a distance of at least 10 kilometres will produce waves about 30 centimetres high after about 2 hours. If it goes on blowing at 10 knots an equilibrium (maximum) height of 50 centimetres will be reached in about 6 hours, so long as the fetch is at least 40 kilometres and the depth greater than 10 metres. Further examples of the heights of newly-generated waves are given in table 17.1. To avoid waves, stay close to a windward shore or island where the fetch is minimal.

Angle between wind and waves
The angle between the wind direction and the wave front makes a significant difference to one's speed through the water, particularly when beating. For the same reason that the surface wind is backed from the pressure gradient wind – friction upsetting the balance of pressure gradient and Coriolis forces – so the wave front lies at an angle of a few degrees back

from the wind producing it in the Northern Hemisphere, and is veered from the wind direction in the Southern Hemisphere. This makes port tack a little faster in the Northern Hemisphere, and starboard tack the faster in the Southern.

However, the wind often changes while the waves are being generated. For instance while a sea breeze is veering there is always a significant angle between the wave front and the wind, and while port tack may be preferable in terms of speed through the water, the veering wind is heading you. Similarly on the passage of a front or trough of low pressure a veer in wind will produce a second set of waves and the sea will be confused. In the 1978 Fastnet storm the wavelength was short both ahead of and behind the cold front because the wind, though very strong, had not been blowing for more than a few hours. The resulting sea was notably confused and dangerous.

Wind and current
If there is a current running against the wind the wavelength shortens while the height remains the same. So the waves become steeper. A strong wind against a strong current produces very steep seas and conditions that are dangerous for all small boats. If at the same time there are shallows, as on a sand bar, the situation is lethal.

When the current runs with the wind the wavelength increases, the sea becomes flatter and sailing much easier and more comfortable. Comparatively small variations in current can sometimes be detected by looking for changes in the wavelength of the waves, particularly in fairly shallow water.

Water temperature
The character of newly produced wind waves depends on the temperature of the surface water compared to the water lower down. If there is a 'slippery' layer of relatively warm water on top of cold the waves will be generated in the warmer

Above: large swell waves obscuring the mark at a Laser World Championship.

water alone, at least to start with, until the wind creates enough mechanical mixing to involve the water lower down. Many times I have heard sailors comment on finding in deep water short steep waves which are characteristic of shallow water. This is because the waves are being generated in a top layer of warm or fresh water, perhaps only a metre or two deep, without involving the water lower down.

Refraction at the shore

When waves approach shallow water they are refracted, because once the depth of water drops to less than half the wavelength, the shallower the water the slower the waves travel. So the wave front bends until it becomes parallel to the shore (figure 17.1).

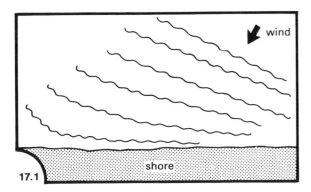

17.1

Swell waves

Larger waves require an adjustment in sailing motion because of the significant variations in boatspeed between the crest and trough of each wave (well described by Lawrie Smith in *Dinghy Helming* in this series). Also they often obscure the marks for a good deal of the time, so make sure you have practised using your compass for navigation.

The most important swell waves are those produced over the wide open ocean. Often generated over a period of several days, they contain a great deal of energy and take as long to decay as they did to develop. Typical values of length and period for waves generated in the Trades are 200 to 300 metres and 12 to 16 seconds. Such waves provide the excellent surfing conditions found on coasts bordering the Atlantic and Pacific Oceans.

As they approach a shore waves always become steeper when the depth of water becomes less than $\frac{1}{25}$ the distance apart of the waves (the wavelength). In the case of swell waves this happens in water of sailing depth, and may make sailing near a lee shore more difficult and possibly dangerous.

Waves as weather predictors

It is useful to recognise that the longer swell waves travel faster than the shorter, locally produced waves, so when they travel ahead of an advancing depression they give advance warning of its approach. The arrival or absence of swell provides a clear distinction between, for instance, an approaching thunderstorm and a deep depression. A threatening sky with increasing black clouds and rain cannot be part of an existing large wind system if there is no swell propagating forwards from it, so any wind must be expected to be temporary. Increasing swell from the direction of advance of the storm clouds suggests an approaching depression with a large area of strong winds coming your way. If there is swell which has been present for a long time without significant change the interpretation is doubtful; for instance the depression may be advancing, but very slowly.

'Freak waves'

Oceanographers usually define the wave height on any patch of water as the height of the one-third highest waves. They call this the 'significant wave height'. You may see this phrase used on a regatta notice board. Some waves will always be smaller than the significant height and some will be bigger. They will often have a variety of lengths and periods too, moving at different speeds and in different directions. So they will be continually overtaking

one another to produce both larger and smaller waves. Every seventh wave is popularly supposed to be bigger than the other six; and statistically you can put a figure to the 1 in 100, 1 in 1000 and so on. In fact a wave twice the significant wave height must be expected every 2000 waves. Wherever you sail you must expect to experience a wave bigger than the rest, so be prepared.

Calm conditions

Ripples here and there are usually evidence of fleeting puffs of wind, but sometimes one area of water appears particularly flat while another nearby looks rather different and suggests the possibility of a light air movement. More often than not such features on the sea surface do not indicate areas of no wind and light wind but variations in movement in the water surface. Where water is subsiding downwards it will appear very flat, sometimes even when there is a faint breath of wind, while where there is upwelling of water the sea surface may appear slightly rippled. Areas of upwelling and subsiding water also suggest horizontal movement, outwards from the upwelling and inwards towards the subsidence.

WIND		WAVE			
speed kt	time blowing	height cm	length metres	min fetch	min depth
10	2 hrs	23	6.9	8km	3.5m
10	6 hrs	50	20.2	40km	10m
20	5 hrs	100	31.6	40km	16m
35	5 hrs	200	56.2	50km	28m
35	20 hrs	600	243	430km	122m

Above: how the size of newly-generated wind waves varies according to the strength of wind and how long it has been blowing, subject to the fetch and depth being greater than the minimum values shown.
Right: the maximum wave height which can be reached for the same wind speeds given sufficient time, fetch and depth.

WIND	WAVE			
speed kt	max ht cm	reached in hrs	fetch km	min depth metres
10	60	8	60	15
20	250	16	240	60
35	750	26	700	170

18 Weather routeing

There is nothing mystical or magical about 'weather routeing'. It is simply making sure that at every stage of a race, however long or short:
1 you have not overlooked any available and relevant weather information and,
2 you have used it to find the quickest way to the finish.

For many years weather routeing was a service provided to commercial shipping on the basis of 'least time, least trouble'; that is, the fastest passage time and minimum risk to cargo and passengers. At the start of the voyage and at regular intervals thereafter the skipper was given a course to steer by a shore-based forecaster using the latest weather information and knowledge of the ship's characteristics.

As the accuracy of weather forecasts up to five days ahead has improved, the techniques of weather routeing have become a realistic option for slower sailing boats on long passages. But it is not a guarantee of success. The routeing advice can only be as good as the forecasts, and the quality of the essential detailed wind information in the forecasts is critically dependent on the quality of the observations on which the forecasts are based.

Short course races
On an Olympic course you have to do your own weather routeing. You need to start with the best and latest shore-based weather information and apply it to the peculiarities of the coast and water, meanwhile observing the minute-by-minute evolution of the weather so you can judge at every stage of the race which is the best way to go.

The same applies in a typical short offshore or inshore race. You will always have a better appreciation of what the wind is doing in the short term, particularly the bends, bands and eddies, than anyone onshore. And the more you appreciate and understand the ways of the wind within the frameworks I have presented in the preceding chapters, the better your judgement will be.

Longer offshore races
So what about the longer offshore races: the Fastnet, for instance, or the Sydney-Hobart? You may find it difficult to believe, but the shore-based forecaster still suffers from the disadvantage that he has not got your view of the weather or your detailed appreciation of what the wind is doing.

Given that you have the basic equipment, including the ability to receive weather broadcasts by radio and fax and a correctly calibrated barometer/barograph so that your observations can be integrated into the weather map, you will normally have an onboard advantage. Take the leg from Bishop Rock to the Fastnet Light. The chance of the shore forecaster having a single ship observation between the Scillies and Southern Ireland is remote – in other words you know more than he does. In a light wind race such as in 1981 and 1991 a forecaster on shore could not have elaborated on his general forecast for sea area Fastnet without weather observations from the yachts.

Long ocean and round-the-world races
This is where weather routeing comes into its own. Whereas in shorter races there is no weather prediction system capable of the accuracy necessary to give consistently good detailed advice from hour to hour, long races require weather knowledge on

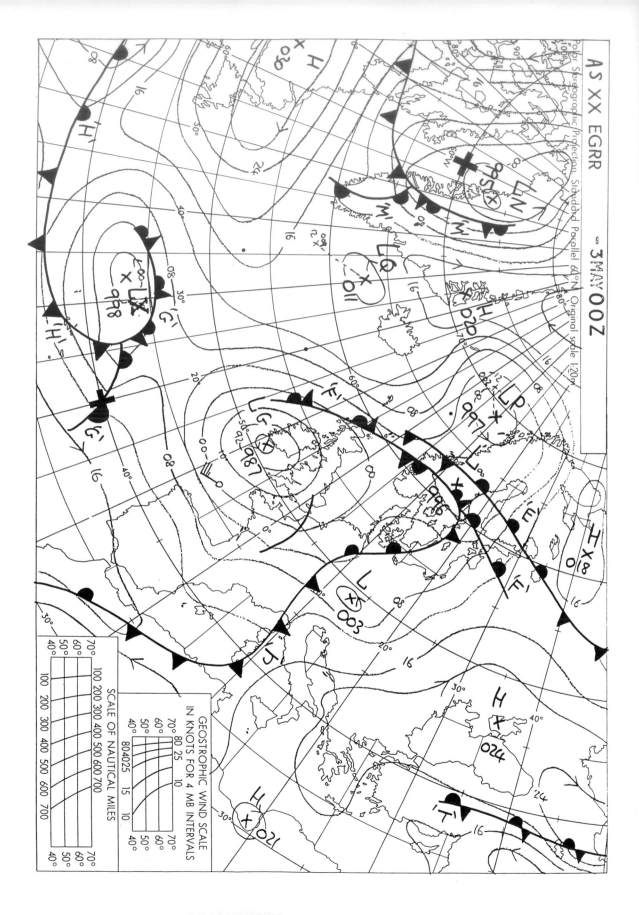

the synoptic scale – which is what all meteorologists major on, and where most progress has been made in recent years.

In its simplest form weather routeing during an ocean race means making sure that you keep on the side of the lows and highs where the winds are the most favourable. Crossing the Atlantic from east to west, for instance, you will want to keep to the north side of the lows or the south side of the highs, and avoid the westerly headwinds in between. If figure 18.1 is typical of the positions of the lows and highs during the race you will route yourself near 50 degrees north over the eastern North Atlantic, dropping down to about 45 degrees north on the western side.

Preparation

Careful, intelligent study of all historical data is an essential part of weather routeing. By 'intelligent' I mean using meteorological common sense such as:
- Realising that charts of average conditions cover a wide range of day-to-day variations which can often be appreciated only from charts showing the tracks of highs and lows
- Realising that historical and actual weather maps and forecasts for data-sparse areas such as the southern oceans are based on incredibly few observations. A published wind rose for a remote ocean grid square may be based on no more than half a dozen ship reports in 50 years!
- Studying available data for coastal stations and thinking it through in terms of the likely sea and land breezes offshore, having due regard to the position of each station: how far it is from the coast and its relationship to features such as mountains and towns. The following illustrations will show you what I mean.

1 Prior to the 1988 sailing Olympics in Pusan, South Korea, data were published for the nearest land station: a very well-equipped meteorological observatory with a 100-year record, only a few miles away from the racing area. But it was on the south slope of a mountain, and sheltered from the north-easterlies which prevailed offshore. The Admiralty pilot gave much better guidance – a brief sentence about north-easterlies.

2 Auckland Airport data are very useful for studying winds over the Hauraki Gulf. But you will get the answer wrong if you do not first look at the topographical map of the area and realise that it lies in a funnel for winds from the south-west.

3 For the Punta del Este to Fort Lauderdale leg of the 1989–90 Whitbread we needed to know whether there might be any advantage in standing in to the South American coast. Data were available for six stations reasonably close to the coast, and interpreting these data in terms of likely land and sea breezes and onshore gradient winds indicated that coastal winds were unreliable. This was confirmed by the odd sentence in the Admiralty pilot. *Ocean Passages of the World* contained an equally brief comment about the best winds being several hundred miles to the east. The information, sparse though it was, was consistent. It was also supported by the five-day forecast received from Bracknell before departure. So *Rothmans* steered a course 700 kilometres east and arrived at Recife with a lead of 300 kilometres.

The Race

Shore-based routeing has the advantage of:
- Frequent pictures from geostationary and polar orbiting satellites, including high resolution pictures, plus skilled interpretation – so long as the shore base is within range of the satellite
- Twice-daily weather forecasts for up to five days ahead – but not always based on very adequate information. Most fax broadcasts receivable on board cover only two days.
- Weather observations from commercial shipping and land stations. This advantage applies mainly to the Atlantic and Pacific trade routes.

On-board routeing has the advantage of:
- Your own continuous appreciation and observation of the weather.
- Always being within range of the appropriate weather satellite. Polar orbiter pictures at low resolution can be picked up on board without significant weight penalty, although their weather forecasting value is questionable.

Any system of routeing can only be as good as the information available in the first place, and on-board computer routeing can suffer from false confidence in the equipment. But there will always be uncertainties, and someone, somewhere has to decide. I doubt whether any system of routeing could prevent boats piling into the sort of wind gate which was met twice in the 1989/90 Whitbread, when the race was virtually restarted. Downwind races will always suffer from this problem, particularly when the boats are making about 15 knots and riding on the backs of the largest weather systems.

◄ 18.1

19 Which sails?

Winning a race can often depend on choosing the right suit of sails for the weather conditions before you go afloat. If you play safe you may lose the race – and if you risk it you may ruin a sail. I am quite sure that the risks can be decreased by sensible application of all the available weather information.

For a first estimate of the wind use the weather forecast. Listen to (or read) as many forecasts as possible for the days before the race to get a feel for the correspondence between the forecast and the actual local wind. Try to judge the reason for differences from the forecast: sea breezes, cliffs, islands, water temperature, etc. Write down the weather map details so that on the day of the race you know the history of all the depressions, anticyclones, troughs and ridges within a few hundred kilometres, and which way they are moving. This information will make a great difference to your appreciation of the forecast, your confidence in it and your own local deductions from it.

Make a practice of looking at the clouds, particularly the lower ones, and judging their speed in relation to the wind you observe on the water. Take a compass bearing on their movement, remembering that for clouds at a height of 300 to 600 metres the direction is about 15 degrees veered (Northern Hemisphere) from the wind on the water. Then even if you are based a few kilometres inland your first observation of the clouds in the morning will tell you a lot about the wind on the nearby water. The surface wind on land early in the day is rarely a guide to the true wind because the surface air at that time is often cold and stable.

Will the wind increase or decrease?
This will depend on whether or not there is a:
- Change in pressure gradient
- Development of a sea breeze
- Change in temperature
- Change in tide
- Band of stronger or lighter wind somewhere on the course.

Change in pressure gradient To judge whether the pressure gradient is changing, use your weather map information. A rough and ready guide is given in the table below.

Wind increasing	Wind decreasing
depression approaching	anticyclone approaching
trough approaching	ridge approaching
anticyclone intensifying	depression filling
depression deepening	anticyclone weakening

Keep an eye on the lower clouds: are they speeding up or slowing down? If so this change will be reflected at the surface. Are the clouds generally increasing or decreasing, suggesting either a trough approaching or a ridge approaching? It also helps to keep an eye on the barometer; a rapid fall of pressure and often a rapid rise indicate increasing winds.

Sea breeze Criteria for judging the development of the sea breeze are given in Chapters 7 and 8 (12 for the Southern Hemisphere).

Change in temperature On inland waters there is a marked change in wind due to a change in land temperature during the day. The wind is at a minimum in the early morning when the surface temperature is lowest and the air most stable. It is at a maximum in the early afternoon when the temperature is highest and the air most unstable.

Out to sea there is often a small change during the day, the water temperature being a degree or so higher in the early afternoon than in the early morning. A rise of even one degree will cause a small decrease in stability and therefore increase the surface wind by perhaps a knot or two.

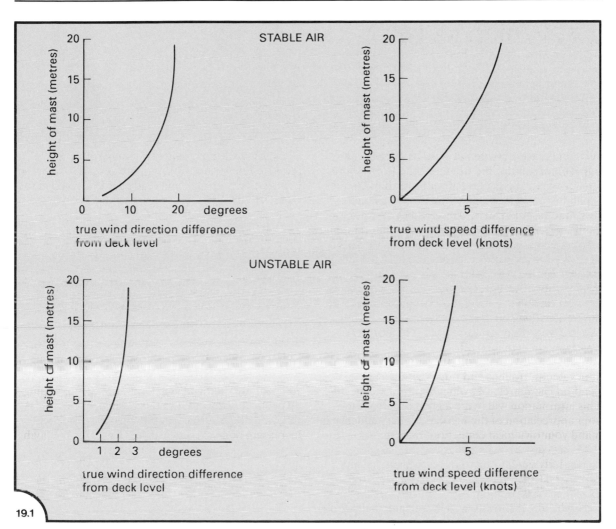

STABLE AIR

true wind direction difference from deck level

true wind speed difference from deck level (knots)

UNSTABLE AIR

true wind direction difference from deck level

true wind speed difference from deck level (knots)

19.1

In coastal waters there is a large variation in offshore winds as the temperature of the land rises and falls during the day. In certain circumstances sea breezes develop. When the gradient is onshore other changes occur which are considered in detail in Chapter 9.

Change in the tide Tide against wind means a relatively rough sea and greater surface friction, therefore less true wind speed. Tide and wind in the same direction means a smoother sea, less friction and a stronger true wind.

Band of stronger or lighter wind This will relate to:
- An island upwind – see Chapter 3.
- A headland upwind – see Chapter 3.
- Wind nearly parallel to the coast – see Chapter 3.
- A slick of warmer or colder water parallel to the wind – see Chapter 4.

Wind shear and weight of wind

We saw in Chapter 2 that friction at the surface changes the direction and strength of the wind compared to higher up. This variation of wind with height is particularly noticeable in the lowest few metres, in fact between deck level and the top of the mast, and is highly dependent on the stability of the air. The comparisons in figure 19.1 are based on instrumental measurements made on a fixed mast over Lough Neagh.

In unstable air (see page 12), when there is a lot of overturning as air warmed at the surface rises to be replaced by colder air from above, the change in wind speed and direction up the mast is small: about 5 per cent and 1 degree. In stable air when there is no overturning it can be as much as 300 per cent in speed and 20 degrees or more in direction. So in stable air (no cumulus, possibly fog) you will need a large amount of twist in your sails on starboard tack, and very closed sails on port tack. In unstable air the leeches can be much straighter. Day-to-day variations in wind shear are particularly noticeable when boardsailing.

A good deal of mystery tends to surround the concept of 'weight of wind'. Time and again one hears the comment after a race that there was more (or less) weight in the wind. Some have tried to attribute the variations to differences in the density of the air, or the water vapour content. But although the density does vary with temperature and the water vapour content rises and falls, these changes are nowhere near sufficient to account for the large observed variations in the 'weight of wind'. They are almost entirely due to variations in wind shear up the mast.

Using the above comparison between the wind speed change up the mast in unstable and stable air, the difference in heeling moment for the same wind speed over the deck is over 50 per cent. Nearly as important is the shear in wind direction, though not in low latitudes – the deflection of the wind due to the Earth's rotation falls to zero at the Equator.

Your judgement regarding the weight of wind depends on whether you are observing the wind at masthead or deck level. Judging from the masthead anemometer reading there will appear to be much more weight in the wind in unstable air, when the wind over the deck will be nearly the same as at the masthead, than in stable air when it will be much lighter. Judging from observations at deck level, and particularly if you assess the wind in relation to the state of the sea surface, the weight of wind will

The shear in wind direction between the lower and upper parts of the sail can be dramatic in stable air.

appear to be greater in stable air when the much stronger wind at the masthead will provide the heeling moment.

20 At the regatta

Where to get weather information

Most regatta managements provide some sort of weather information service for a race series. Pinned on a notice board somewhere you will probably find an 'actual' weather map for midnight or 0600 GMT on the day of the race, a forecast weather map for 12 or 24 hours later, and a written forecast for the race area. You may see a chart with code letters in one corner. The most common are 'AS' meaning actual surface and 'FS' meaning forecast surface. The letter 'U' denotes an upper air chart.

Telephone and radio weather services may also be convenient. Details (for Europe) of numbers, frequencies and times are given in the RYA booklet G5 *Weather Forecasts* which I wrote and update every year. The Marinecall service in the UK is one of the best.

Is the weather forecast useful?

Many is the time I have heard a frustrated helmsman blame the forecast for his poor position at the windward or leeward mark, and indeed there is no better scapegoat. But is a standard forecast or even a specialist forecast for the race area of much help? Occasionally, of course, it will be dead right and there will be someone who has believed it and won. But what about on average?

A blind, uncritical and unintelligent application of the weather forecast is worse than useless. For one thing, the majority of forecasts are not prepared specifically for the area and time of the race. A land area forecast is not designed for the inland or coastal sailor, nor is a shipping bulletin. And quite often you will find that a forecast specifically designed for the regatta has been prepared by someone without the necessary knowledge of coastal wind behaviour.

Another thing to guard against is the blind application of information given about movements of major systems such as fronts, troughs and ridges. The chance of one of these crossing the area during a race is small, and the chance of predicting the time of an associated windshift to within 20 minutes, or getting it right on a particular beat, is almost nil.

That said, the weather forecast is a vital piece of information for every sailor in every regatta. Its value lies in the background information which it provides: information which will enable you to judge the likelihood, position and character of bends, bands and shifts in the wind. In fact you cannot apply the information in Chapters 2 to 19 unless you know which is the gradient wind and how it is expected to change – information that is the basic ingredient of every forecast.

Can anything be gleaned from satellite pictures?

A copy of the latest picture from a weather satellite may be displayed or included in a handout. This helps to give credibility to the diagrammatic weather map: you can see for yourself that there are real swirls of cloud – depressions – and long, broad bands of cloud – fronts. But the pictures lack the resolution necessary to tell you anything useful about local cloud structures, while to deduce anything about their associated winds requires specialist expertise and a great deal of practice. So the answer is "no" – but they are nice to look at.

The importance of your own observations

I am always amazed how many sailors either rely on what they are told and ignore what they can see for themselves, or rely on what they can see happening before a regatta and ignore the forecast and the indications of change. Your own observation is a piece in the weather jigsaw which is likely to be unique to you, and not available to the forecaster operating at a weather centre some distance away. Your observations are weather *facts,* and every forecast is based on the *facts* about the weather at the time it was written. Never throw either the forecast or observation out of the window. The more you practise putting them together the better will be your judgement in a race.

During the previous few days
Follow the weather on the scale of the weather map Note the movements of depressions, fronts, troughs, anticyclones and ridges from day to day, using the charts in the daily newspapers or on television. Get a feel for how fast things are moving and developing and for the way the pressure gradient wind is changing from day to day in both speed and direction.

Follow the weather on the small scale If you are preparing the boat near the regatta area, practise following the clouds and the wind variations, getting a feel for the changes as they occur. Try to distinguish events which are due solely to changes in the gradient wind and those which are due to local factors.

Study the course Think out the likely sea breezes for different gradient wind directions. Consider what effects the land will have on the wind if it is blowing offshore. Are there islands, bays and other features to influence the wind? What is the water temperature? Is it uniform? Are there are rivers – sources of fresh water – nearby? Look up the tides and the general currents for the area.

The morning of the race
Ask yourself these questions:
- What is the gradient wind doing, both in direction and speed? How does it tie in with the movement of the pressure systems over the past few days? What is it forecast to do over the next few hours? If you have no access to a weather map you will have to judge the gradient wind from the forecast surface wind: assume that it is in approximately the same direction if the forecast uses an eight-point compass, or veered by 15 degrees if you have more detail.
- How are the low clouds moving? Take a compass bearing on their direction and judge their speed. Does their movement fit the forecast? If it does not, then either mountains or valleys are interfering with it (see page 56) or you listened to the wrong forecast.
- What surface wind have you at present? Is it the remains of a night land breeze? (see Chapter 11). Has it been killed by a night-time temperature inversion? (see pages 12 and 34). Or does it agree with the gradient wind: 40 degrees or so back from it over land and much lighter early in the day? Details of land breezes and other local winds are not

normally covered in a standard weather forecast. Refer to Chapters 11 and 13 to sort them out.
- What wind is forecast over the water? Does the forecast appear to have taken into account coastal influences on the wind? The standard sea area forecast for shipping does not normally include coastal effects, but it provides essential background information which you can easily translate into what the gradient wind is expected to do. The rest you may have to work out for yourself.
- Is the wind nearly parallel to the coast? If it is, you must consider the divergence or convergence of streamlines (see figures 3.6 and 3.8).
- Has the gradient wind an offshore component – i.e. is it in quadrants 1 or 2? If it is less than 25 knots and cloud is thin or broken expect a sea breeze (see Chapter 7, 8 or 12). If it is strong or you are racing before or after the sea breeze expect a bend or standing waves (see Chapter 3 or 6).
- Has the gradient wind an onshore component – i.e. is it in quadrants 3 or 4? See Chapter 9 or 12 for what happens when the land heats up, Chapters 3, 11 and 12 for other times.
- Are there islands upwind? (see Chapter 3 or 6).
- Is the air stable, with flat low cloud or hazy – or unstable, with cumulus clouds and good visibility? Think of gusts and lulls (Chapter 5) or possible bands (Chapters 4 and 14).
- Are showers likely? See figure 14.2 for wind associated with a raining cloud.
- Is there a current running? See flow chart on page 71.

Sailing to the start
Observe and record the windshifts. Note any changes in cloud.
- Is the cloud dispersing just offshore? This suggests that a sea breeze is about to appear (see Chapter 8).
- Is the cloud generally increasing to weather? This suggests the approach of a trough – see 'lines of cloud' on page 65.
- Is the cloud developing only over the land? This suggests a sea breeze building if the gradient wind is in quadrant 1 or 2 (Chapter 8); other and possibly very different thermal influences if the gradient is in quadrant 3 or 4 (Chapter 9).

Before the start
- Is there a bias on the line?
- What will the bias be at the time of the start?

See pages 26 and 28 for the timing of gusts and lulls. See Chapters 8 and 9 for guidance on how far the wind direction swings in different situations.

On the first beat

Does one side pay? If so is this due to:

- Features of the land or islands affecting the wind? (Chapter 3).
- The presence of a sea breeze? (Chapters 7 and 8).
- Water temperature variations across or upwind of the course? (Chapter 4).
- Current or tide differences across the course? (Chapter 16).

If there is a good reason for one side paying, and you expect that feature of the wind or water to persist, go towards that side next time around. How far you should go towards the lay line will depend on how certain you are that the bias is permanent. For instance, if there is an island upwind and no change in wind direction you can be confident that the bands of strong and light wind downwind from the island will continue. If you can find no good reason for the bias then go up the middle next time and play the shifts.

Deduce your own forecast – example

Geography: flat coast facing east.
Race area: circle 5 kilometres in diameter, 2 to 7 kilometres from the shore.
Complications: island 3 kilometres diameter, 5 kilometres north of race area.
Tides and currents: tide only – normally no other current.
Weather past few days: succession of fronts and troughs moving eastwards. Wind force 6 previous day.
General forecast for area (from radio or TV): trough approaching from west during evening; wind south-west force 2 to 3 backing southerly and increasing force 5 to 6 by evening. Rain later. Local sea breeze near coast for a time.
Weather at breakfast time: sunny – no cloud.
Morning gradient wind: there is no low cloud to indicate the direction of the gradient wind so you must infer this from the 'official' forecast. A south-westerly surface wind over the water implies a gradient wind about WSW.
Time of start: 1300.
Forecast gradient wind in afternoon: forecast wind backing southerly so the gradient wind must back towards SSW.

Cloud increasing ahead of a trough of low pressure.

Likelihood of sea breeze: no mention of sea breeze direction or strength in the forecast but the gradient wind is in quadrant 1, and although backing a little will stay in this quadrant. So a good sea breeze expected so long as the land is warmer than the water, i.e. until general cloud arrives ahead of the trough.
Your wind forecast: wind south-westerly force 2 to 3 at first, dying as easterly sea breeze sets in over the race area before midday. Sea breeze at start of race probably ESE force 1 to 2 increasing and veering to SSE force 3 to 4. If general increase in cloud then gradient wind probably taking control causing veer to southerly, perhaps up to force 5 by late afternoon. Full effect of gradient wind will not be experienced near the coast since airstreams on land and water will be diverging.
Possible complications:
Wind – island is downwind of race area so it has no effect.
Current – water well mixed (force 6 previous day) so no wind-driven surface current expected. Coastline uncomplicated so no eddies.
Gusts – sea breeze air is normally stable, so no short tack gust-lull sequence likely. Longer period swings are often experienced in this situation with 'gusts' usually from the direction towards which the wind is changing, in this case a veer.

21 Some popular venues

DUBLIN BAY

Gradient wind 180 to 200 degrees

Morning surface wind over water around 165 to 185 degrees. Afternoon heating over land will cause gradient near coast to back until isobars are parallel to the shore. Wind over water will swing to about 165 degrees and increase by about 5 knots. Look for slight bend into bay (figure 21.1).

Gradient wind 120 to 170 degrees

Morning surface wind over water around 105 to 155 degrees. Afternoon heating over land will cause gradient near coast to veer until isobars are more aligned to coast, with 5 ot 6-knot increase in speed. Direction on water will swing towards but not beyond 165 degrees (figure 21.1).

Gradient wind in quadrant 1, less than 20 knots

Morning wind on water south-westerly. Sea breeze to be expected unless very cloudy. Wind will die over water from mid-morning with onshore sea breeze starting to close in, extending steadily seawards and building. Direction will swing to the right towards a final value of about 160 degrees, except in the bay itself where it will bend towards the shore to get around the mountains (figure 21.2).

Gradient wind in quadrant 2, less than 15 knots

Morning wind on water north-westerly. Sea breeze to be expected unless very cloudy; starting 4 to 8 kilometres seaward of the shore, extending slowly shorewards and more quickly seawards. Shoreward edge of sea breeze marked by thicker cloud and moving erratically; probably making better progress on north side of Dublin Bay (figure 21.3).

Gradient wind offshore and over about 25 knots

No sea breeze. Heating of the land causes an increase in buoyancy over the land so the surface wind increases, with gusts approaching gradient wind speed and direction. Wind near the shore will reflect these changes in the land wind. Lulls will be more pronounced – lighter and more backed – the nearer you are to the shore.

Gradient wind between 360 and 120 degrees

For surface wind between 005 and 025 degrees, expect a band of stronger wind along coast north of Howth extending across the isthmus into Dublin Bay, and another just east of Howth Head (figure 21.4).

For surface wind between 100 and 120 degrees expect a band of stronger wind just south of Howth Head with a light band on the opposite side of the bay. Dublin Bay is just the right size to accommodate a fully-developed strong band on one side and a light band on the other (figure 21.5).

Expect wind to be lighter in the afternoon for directions between north-east and north.

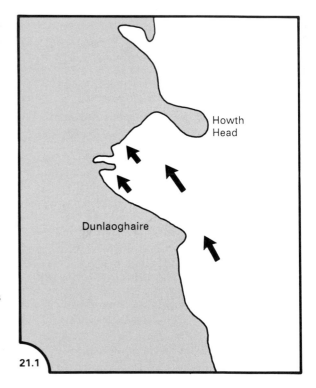

Howth
Head

Dunlaoghaire

21.1

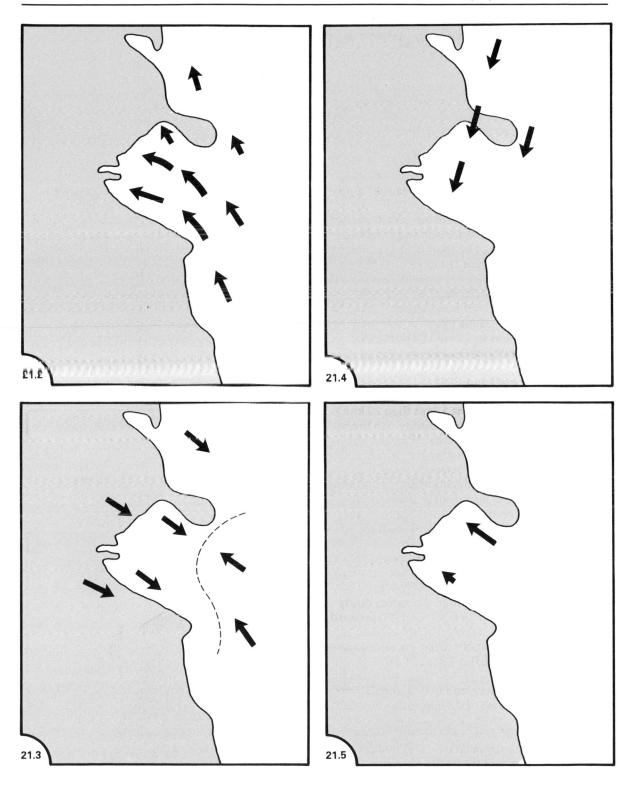

21.2

21.4

21.3

21.5

THE SOLENT

Applying the rules and guidelines of Chapters 3, 8, 9, and 10 to the Solent is not as confusing as you might imagine. For each stretch of coast you look for bends and bands in the wind related to the alignment of the wind with that particular coast. These are summarised in figures 21.6 to 21.9. Wind bands generated on one stretch of coast will extend a long way downwind if free to do so. The best example of this is the band of strong wind generated on the west shore of Southampton Water extending way down the east Solent.

Similarly whether or not a sea breeze will develop will depend on the direction and strength of the gradient wind. This too can be worked out. Whether the breeze can be sustained will depend on the size of the land or water area available to it. The first two to three hours of its development are inevitably complex, so guidance on this is provided in figure 7.6.

The general pattern for the afternoon can be summarised as follows:

Early morning wind	Afternoon wind
between west and north	fresh south-westerly sea breeze
between SSW and WSW	increase by one force; little change in direction
between south and ESE	decrease by one force
between east and NNE	south-westerly sea breeze struggling to move in from seawards, but may not reach mainland shore particularly in east Solent.

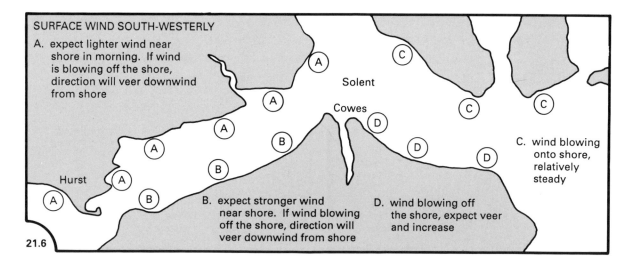

SURFACE WIND SOUTH-WESTERLY

A. expect lighter wind near shore in morning. If wind is blowing off the shore, direction will veer downwind from shore

B. expect stronger wind near shore. If wind blowing off the shore, direction will veer downwind from shore

C. wind blowing onto shore, relatively steady

D. wind blowing off the shore, expect veer and increase

Solent
Cowes
Hurst

21.6

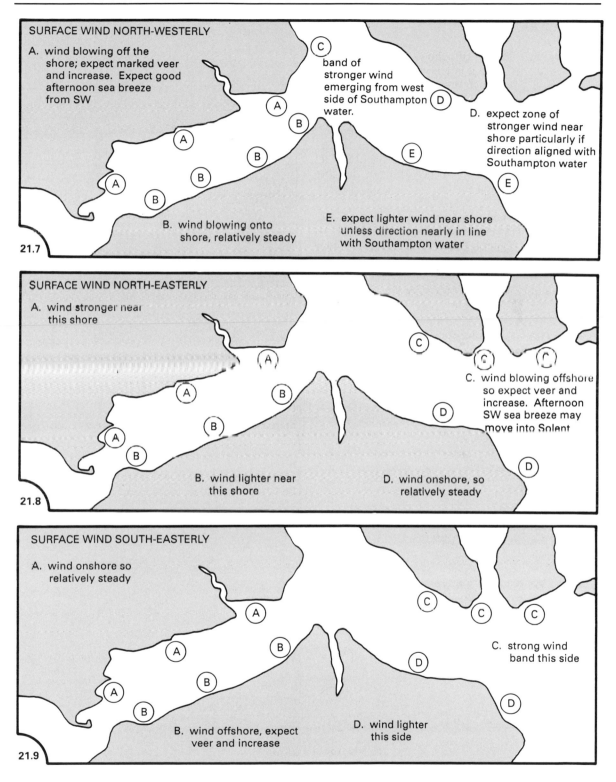

SURFACE WIND NORTH-WESTERLY

A. wind blowing off the shore; expect marked veer and increase. Expect good afternoon sea breeze from SW

C. band of stronger wind emerging from west side of Southampton water.

D. expect zone of stronger wind near shore particularly if direction aligned with Southampton water

B. wind blowing onto shore, relatively steady

E. expect lighter wind near shore unless direction nearly in line with Southampton water

21.7

SURFACE WIND NORTH-EASTERLY

A. wind stronger near this shore

C. wind blowing offshore so expect veer and increase. Afternoon SW sea breeze may move into Solent

B. wind lighter near this shore

D. wind onshore, so relatively steady

21.8

SURFACE WIND SOUTH-EASTERLY

A. wind onshore so relatively steady

C. strong wind band this side

B. wind offshore, expect veer and increase

D. wind lighter this side

21.9

KIEL

Gradient wind 010 to 100 degrees

Wind over water in range 350 to 080 degrees. If Als or other land upwind (surface wind) look for a band of stronger wind trailing downwind over the course area; though if windspeed less than 10 knots expect breakaway eddies instead. Effect of afternoon heating of the land likely to be noticeable only if surface wind light and between about 350 and 020 degrees.

Gradient wind 100 to 160 degrees

Morning wind on water east to south-easterly. Afternoon wind will be enhanced by 5 to 10 knots due to heating of the land and direction will change (back or veer) towards the direction shown in figure 21.10, with a bend to the coast particularly on the right-hand side of the beat.

Gradient wind 160 to 250 degrees

i) gradient less than about 20 knots, sunny over land or only thin or patchy cloud. Arrows in figure 21.11 indicate initial stages of sea breeze development. However, details depend on the angle of the initial (offshore) wind to the coast, e.g. when the gradient is in the south-west the sea breeze will start close to the coast near the course area and spread steadily seawards.

Arrows in figure 21.12 show likely pattern of afternoon sea breeze. Sea breeze strongest inshore (arrows proportional to strength).

ii) gradient over 20 knots and sunny, or light gradient and cloudy. Expect offshore wind to continue, but with swings and holes due to occasional attempts at sea breeze.

Gradient wind 260 to 290 degrees

Morning wind on water between south-west and west. Sea breeze generation will be preferentially onto the shores to the south-west and north-west of the area. Arrows in figure 21.13 show likely flow of developed sea breeze.

Gradient wind 290 to 010 degrees

Expect gusts and swings in the wind due to influence of land and fjords. Look for bands of stronger wind downwind of coastal features lying along the wind.

If gradient between 290 and 310 degrees look for sea breeze influences: a) on landward (SW) side of course (see figure 21.13); b) on NW side of course as sea breeze onto land north of Eckenforde extends seawards.

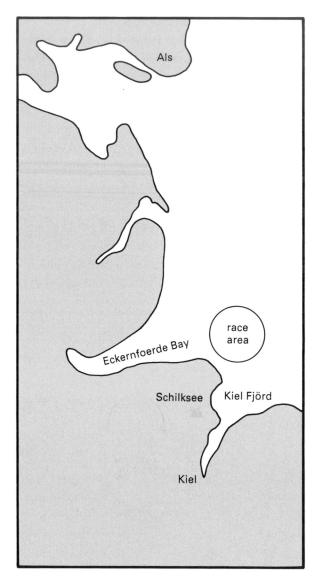

The race area at Kiel in relation to the local coastline.

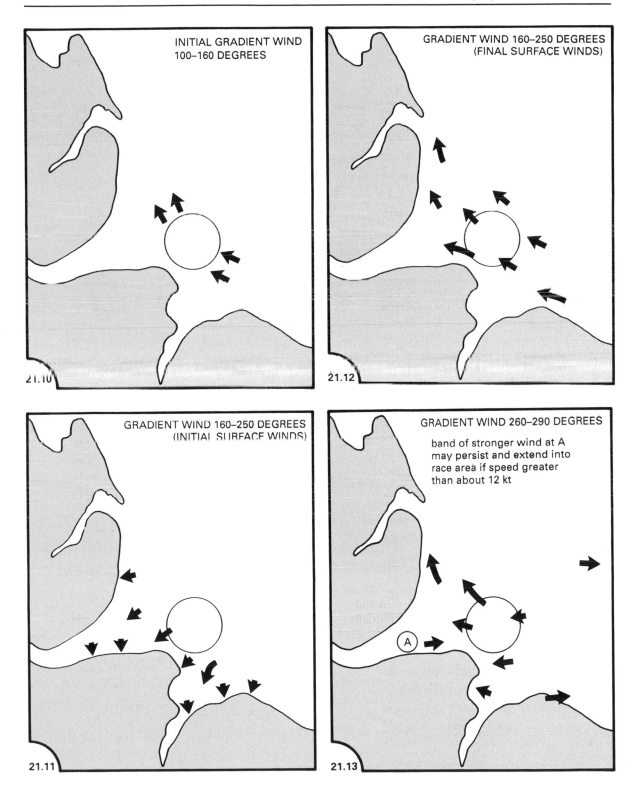

INITIAL GRADIENT WIND
100–160 DEGREES

21.10

GRADIENT WIND 160–250 DEGREES
(FINAL SURFACE WINDS)

21.12

GRADIENT WIND 160–250 DEGREES
(INITIAL SURFACE WINDS)

21.11

GRADIENT WIND 260–290 DEGREES

band of stronger wind at A
may persist and extend into
race area if speed greater
than about 12 kt

A

21.13

BARCELONA

Winds at Barcelona in the summer six months of the year follow a pattern typical of places:
- on a relatively straight coast;
- where an adjacent large land mass becomes hot in the afternoon (but not in the tropics);
- where gradient winds are normally light.

The following analysis and discussion focuses on Barcelona, but can be applied similarly to places like Anzio, Cannes, Fremantle, Los Angeles, Palamos, San Diego.

Morning gradient wind less than 2 or 3 knots – any direction

The morning starts calm and the air aloft is drifting around from no direction in particular. Heating of the land causes the pressure to fall overland and an along-shore gradient wind sets in by midday. Typical features of the wind on the water are as follows:
- It starts before mid-morning as a pure sea breeze at right angles to the coast (from 140 degrees at Barcelona), which swings to the right and increases for a while.
- The thermally-produced gradient parallel to the

coast then takes over, pulling the direction round to 15 degrees from the shoreline by early afternoon (195 degrees at Barcelona), with a slight bend inshore near to the shore.
- At the same time the speed increases to around 10 knots over a coastal zone about 5 to 8 kilometres wide.
- Swings in a direction between 195 and 220 degrees arise from interactions with the wind produced beyond a bend in the coast upwind.

Gradient wind in quadrant 3

It often happens that the morning starts with a remnant of the southerly wind of the previous day, in which case the final direction and the swings are the same as above but the speed is 5 knots or so higher. South-easterly winds also swing right but not so far, and with only 2 or 3 knots increase in speed.

Westerly gradient – quadrant 1

A quadrant 1 gradient wind is a fairly common occurrence at Fremantle (where it is a south-easterly) but relatively infrequent on Californian and Mediterranean coasts. At Barcelona it is most likely following the passage of a cold front – usually

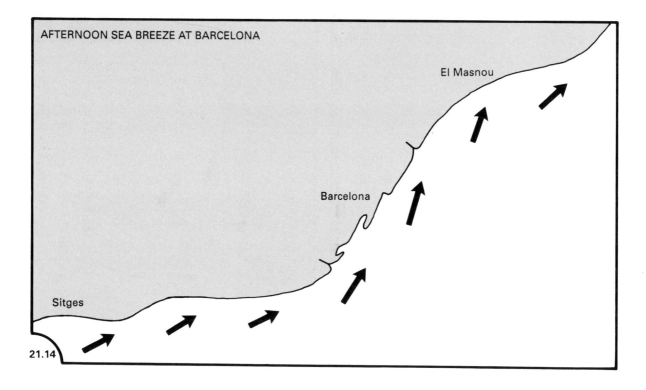

AFTERNOON SEA BREEZE AT BARCELONA

El Masnou

Barcelona

Sitges

21.14

so weak that it is barely recognisable except for the change to much clearer air. A sea breeze sets in early, extends seawards, swings to about 210 degrees and increases to 20 or 25 knots near the shore. The direction fluctuates between 210 and 225 degrees because interaction with the breeze upwind around the corner (figure 21.14).

East to north-east gradient – quadrant 4

A morning wind over the water between about 020 and 100 degrees is usually killed by the opposing thermal vector. But if it is less than about 5 or 6 knots it ends up (either pulled round or stopped and started again) at about 160 to 180 degrees with probably a small increase in speed. On some coasts a true sea breeze follows the death of the initial wind but it is rare to find this happening at Barcelona.

Northerly gradient – quadrant 2

This is rarely if ever found in summer at Barcelona because of the Pyrenees.

TRAVEMUNDE

Lubeck Bay is fairly typical of a racing area with land on three sides. Winds from the north-east entering the open end of the bay are influenced by the coasts to right and left according to the normal rules (figures 3.6 and 3.8). When gradient winds are blowing off either the north-west or south-east coasts on a sunny day you can work out the development and evolution of the sea breeze by asking the question "where is the air coming from to feed it?". The closed end of the bay is obviously not a good source.

Figure 21.15 illustrates the sort of wind pattern to be found two or three hours after the start of the sea breeze when the gradient wind is in the north-west. For a south-easterly gradient the patterns are similar, in reverse. The length of the arrows is roughly proportional to the strength of the wind, but no precise relationship is intended.

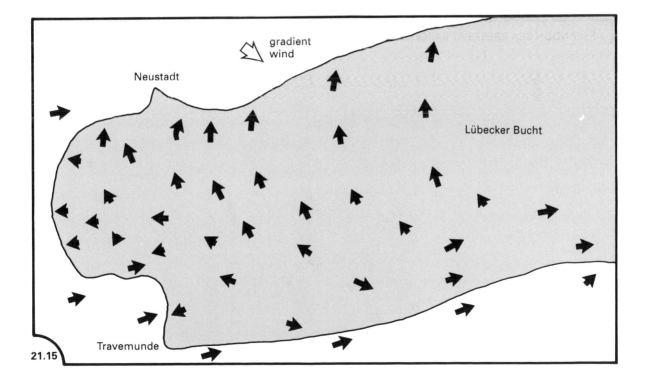

21.15

Index

Alongshore wind   18
Anzio   90

Back(ing) wind   10
Barcelona   90
Barrier effects   67
Billows   58
Buoyancy   10, 12
Buys Ballots Law   9

Cannes   90
Cloud bands   62
Cloud streets   65
Coastal cliffs   20
Cold surge   58
Convergence   18
Coriolis Force   10
Cumulus   10

Divergence   19
Drag   10
Dublin Bay   84

Evening winds   51

Fetch   72
Fog   66
Freak waves   74
Fremantle   90
Fremantle Doctor   55
Friction   9

Geostrophic scale   9
Geostrophic wind   9
Gradient wind   9
Gradient wind and sea breeze   39
Gravity waves   58
Gust   14, 26, 32

Inversion   34

Kelvin-Helmholtz Waves   58
Kiel   88

Lake breeze   36, 48
Land breeze   51
Los Angeles   90
Lull   14, 26, 32

Offshore wind   16
Onshore wind   20

Peninsular winds   48
Pressure gradient   9

Quadrants   40

Refraction   73

San Diego   90
Satellite pictures   81
Sea breeze   34
Sea breeze calms   42
Sea breeze eddy   52
Solent   86
Stability (of air)   10, 12, 79
Standing waves   20
Subsidence   34
Swell   73

Thunderstorm winds   62
Thunderstorm safety   62

Unstable air   12

Valley wind   56
Veer   10
Vortex rolls   23

Weather map   9
Weather routeing   75
Weight of wind   79
Wind bands   23
Wind shear   66, 79
Wind waves   72

Winds near coasts

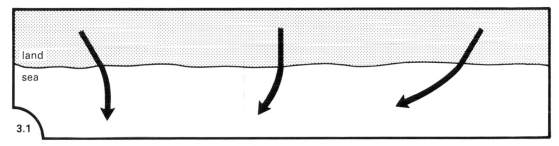

3.1

Above: with the wind blowing off the shore the wind veers and increases. On a gusty day the changes are most apparent in the lulls.

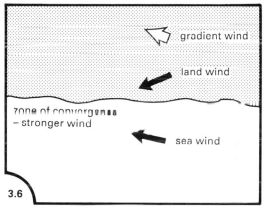

land wind

gradient wind

zone of convergence
– stronger wind

sea wind

3.6

Above: with a wind blowing along the shore and the land on your right (with your back to the wind) expect a band of up to 25% stronger wind 1–5 km offshore.

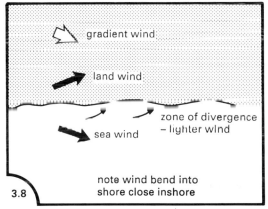

gradient wind

land wind

zone of divergence
– lighter wind

sea wind

note wind bend into
shore close inshore

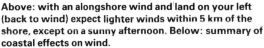

3.8

Above: with an alongshore wind and land on your left (back to wind) expect lighter winds within 5 km of the shore, except on a sunny afternoon. Below: summary of coastal effects on wind.

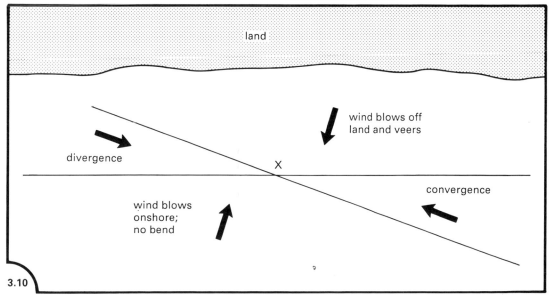

land

divergence

wind blows off
land and veers

X

convergence

wind blows
onshore;
no bend

3.10

Influence of other features on the wind

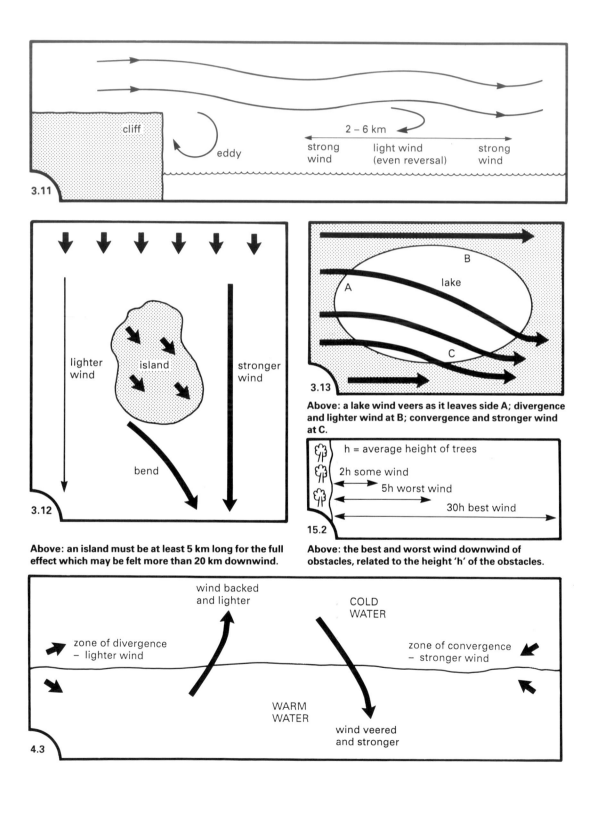

3.11

cliff

eddy

2 – 6 km

strong wind

light wind (even reversal)

strong wind

3.12

lighter wind

island

stronger wind

bend

Above: an island must be at least 5 km long for the full effect which may be felt more than 20 km downwind.

3.13

B

A

lake

C

Above: a lake wind veers as it leaves side A; divergence and lighter wind at B; convergence and stronger wind at C.

15.2

h = average height of trees

2h some wind

5h worst wind

30h best wind

Above: the best and worst wind downwind of obstacles, related to the height 'h' of the obstacles.

4.3

wind backed and lighter

COLD WATER

zone of divergence – lighter wind

zone of convergence – stronger wind

WARM WATER

wind veered and stronger

The sea breeze

Summary and signs
- Clear morning sky, or thin cloud.
- Temperature over land rises above sea temperature.
- Cloud offshore begins to dissolve.
- Initial offshore wind, if any, dies inshore.
- Gentle drift starts on to shore.
- Breeze builds and extends seawards, preceded by calm zone separating initial wind and sea breeze.
- Cloud over land, if any, more cumuliform.
- Breeze veers some 40 degrees in first hour then more slowly until 20 degrees back from shoreline.
- Strength increases; maximum force 4 or 5 always near the shore.
- Breeze dies towards sunset.

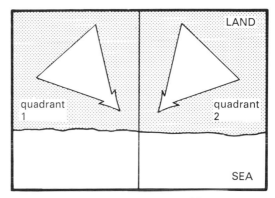

Above: the sea breeze quadrants 1 and 2.

Below: the development of the sea breeze with a quadrant 1 gradient wind. Quadrant 2 is shown overleaf.

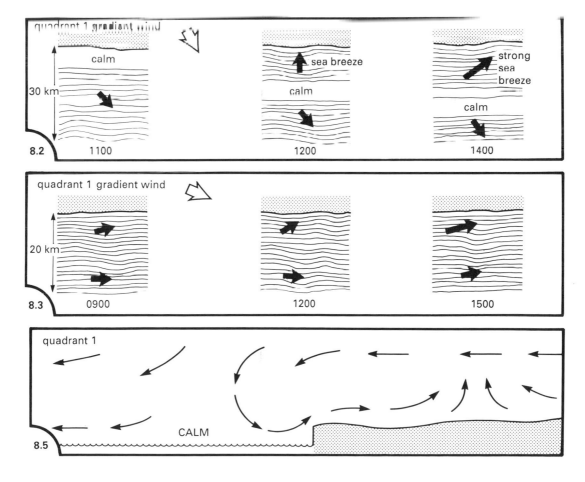

Sea breeze continued . . .

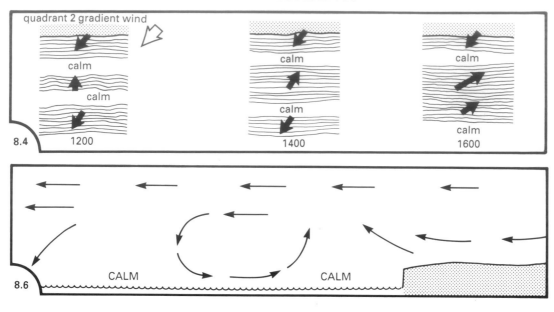

quadrant 2 gradient wind

8.4   1200   1400   1600

8.6   CALM   CALM

Afternoon wind with gradient wind onshore

Heating of the land causes a fall of pressure which adds a component of wind of 4 or 5 knots parallel to the coast. This augments a quadrant 3 wind, especially if it is nearly parallel to the coast, but tends to kill a quadrant 4 wind.

The major differences between the enhancement of a quadrant 3 wind and a true sea breeze are:
- The full benefit of the thermal enhancement is achieved only when the morning wind is within about 20 degrees from the line of the coast.
- The increase in speed is spread over a zone several kilometres wide.
- The change in direction depends on the strength and direction of the initial wind. It may be only a few degrees.

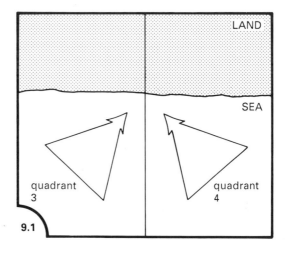

LAND

SEA

quadrant 3   quadrant 4

9.1

Will the wind increase or decrease?
Check whether there will be:
- A change in pressure gradient.
- Development of a sea breeze (offshore gradient).
- Thermal enhancement or reduction of an onshore wind.
- A change in tide.
- A band of stronger or lighter wind.

If one side pays on a beat is it due to?
- A feature of the land or an island upwind.
- A sea breeze.
- Water temperature variations across or upwind of the course.
- Current or tide variations.